2000
SHORTHAND

Pocket
Dictionary

Second Edition

LONGMAN

Addison Wesley Longman Limited
Edinburgh Gate, Harlow
Essex CM20 2JE, England
and Associated Companies throughout the world

First Published 1978
Second Edition 1983
Reprinted 1983, 1984, 1985 (twice), 1987, 1988, 1990, 1992, 1993, 1994
Reprinted by Longman Group Limited 1995,
Reprinted by Addison Wesley Longman Limited 1996, 1997

British Library Cataloguing in Publication Data
A catalogue entry for this title is available from the British Library.

ISBN 0-582-28722-7

Library of Congress Cataloging-in-Publication Data
A catalog entry for this title is available from the Library of Congress.

Printed in Singapore

PREFACE

The Pitman 2000 Shorthand Pocket Dictionary is designed to provide, in a size suitable for pocket use, a guide to the shorthand outlines for the more common words in the English language. The shorthand outlines in this work are not always necessarily the only theoretically correct ones. The outlines show position writing and are given in vocalised shorthand. All the short forms and derivatives are shown italicized.

A

a	ablaze'
aback'	a'ble
aban'don	a'ble-bodied
aban'doned	ablu'tion
aban'doning	a'bly
aban'donment	abnor'mal
abash'	abnormal'ity
abashed'	aboard'
abate'	abode'
aba'ted	abol'ish
abate'ment	abol'ished
abat'ing	abol'ishing
abattoir'	abol'ishment
ab'bot	aboli'tion
abbre'viate	abom'inable
abbre'viated	abom'inate
abbre'viating	abom'inated
abbrevia'tion	abomina'tion
ab'dicate	aborig'inal
ab'dicated	abor'tive
ab'dicating	abound'
abdica'tion	abound'ed
abdo'men	abound'ing
abdom'inal	about'
abduct'	above'
abduct'ed	abra'sion
abduct'ing	abreast'
abduc'tion	abridge'
aberra'tion	abridged'
abey'ance	abridg'ing
abhor'	abridg'ment
abhorred'	abroad'
abhor'rence	ab'rogate
abhor'rent	abroga'tion
abhor'ring	abrupt'
abide'	abrupt'ly
abid'ing	abrupt'ness
abil'ity	ab'scess
ab'ject	abscond'
ab'jectly	abscond'ed

5

abscond'er
abscond'ing
ab'sence
(ab'sent, *a.*
(absent', *v.*
absent'ed
absentee'
ab'solute
ab'solutely
absolu'tion
absolve'
absorb'
absorbed'
absorb'ent
absorb'ing
absorp'tion
abstain'
abstain'er
abstain'ing
abste'mious
absten'tion
ab'stinence
(abstract', *v.*
(ab'stract,
   a. & *n.*
abstract'ed
abstract'ing
abstrac'tion
abstruse'
absurd'
absurd'ity
absurd'ly
abun'dance
abun'dant
abun'dantly
abuse'
abused'
abus'ing
abu'sive
abu'sively
abut'
abyss'
academ'ic
academ'ical
acad'emy
accede'
acced'ed
acced'ing

accel'erate
accel'erated
accel'erating
accelera'tion
accel'erator
(ac'cent, *n.*
(accent', *v.*
accent'ed
accent'ing
accent'uate
accent'uated
accentua'tion
accept'
accept'able
accept'ance
accept'ed
accept'ing
ac'cess
accessibil'ity
acces'sible
acces'sion
ac'cessory
ac'cident
acciden'tal
acclaim'
acclama'tion
accli'matize
accli'matized
accli'matizing
accom'modate
accom'modated
accom'modat-
   ing
accommoda'-
   tion
accom'panied
accom'pani-
   ment
accom'panist
accom'pany
accom'panying
accom'plice
accom'plish
accom'plished
accom'plishing
accom'plish-
   ment
accord'

accord'ance	ac'me	
accord'ed	a'corn	
accord'ing	acous'tic	
accord'ingly	acquaint'	
accord'ion	acquaint'ance	
account'	acquaint'ed	
account'able	acquaint'ing	
account'ancy	acquiesce'	
account'ant	acquies'cence	
account'ed	acquire'	
account'ing	acquired'	
accred'ited	acquire'ment	
accre'tion	acquir'ing	
accrue'	acquisi'tion	
accrued'	acquis'itive	
accru'ing	acquit'	
accu'mulate	acquit'tal	
accu'mulated	acquit'ted	
accu'mulating	acquit'ting	
accumula'tion	a'cre	
accu'mulator	a'creage	
ac'curacy	ac'rid	
ac'curate	acrimo'nious	
ac'curately	ac'robat	
accusa'tion	acrobat'ic	
accuse'	ac'ronym	
accused'	across'	
accus'ing	act	
accus'tom	act'ed	
accus'tomed	act'ing	
ace	actin'ium	
acerb'ity	ac'tion	
acet'ylene	ac'tionable	
ache	ac'tivate	
ached	ac'tive	
achieve'	ac'tively	
achieved'	activ'ity	
achieve'ment	act'or	
achiev'ing	act'ress	
ach'ing	act'ual	
ac'id	act'ually	
acid'ity	act'uary	
acidos'is	acu'ity	
acknowl'edge	acu'men	
acknowl'edged	acute'	
acknowl'edging	acute'ly	
acknowl'edg-	ad'age	
ment	ad'amant	

adapt'		
adaptabil'ity		
adapt'able		
adapta'tion		
adapt'ed		
adapt'ing		
add		
ad'ded		
addict'		
addic'ted		
ad'ding		
addi'tion		
addi'tional		
address'		
addressed'		
addressee'		
address'ing		
adept'		
ad'equacy		
ad'equate		
ad'equately		
adhere'		
adhered'		
adhe'rence		
adhe'rent		
adhe'ring		
adhe'sion		
adhe'sive		
adhe'siveness		
adieu'		
adja'cent		
adja'cently		
ad'jective		
adjoin'		
adjoin'ing		
adjourn'		
adjourned'		
adjourn'ing		
adjourn'ment		
adju'dicate		
adjudica'tion		
ad'junct		
adjust'		
adjust'ed		
adjust'ing		
adjust'ment		
admin'ister		
admin'istered		

admin'istering		
admin'istrate		
administra'- tion		
admin'istra- tive		
admin'istrator		
ad'mirable		
ad'miral		
ad'miralty		
admira'tion		
admire'		
admired'		
admir'er		
admir'ing		
admir'ingly		
admis'sible		
admis'sion		
admit'		
admit'tance		
admit'ted		
admit'ting		
admon'ish		
admon'ished		
admon'ishing		
admoni'tion		
adoles'cence		
adoles'cent		
adopt'		
adopt'ed		
adopt'ing		
adop'tion		
ador'able		
adora'tion		
adore'		
ador'ing		
adorn'		
adorned'		
adorn'ing		
adorn'ment		
adre'nal		
adren'alin		
adult'		
adul'terate		
adul'terated		
adultera'tion		
adult'hood		
advance'		

advanced'	affect'
advance'ment	affecta'tion
advan'cing	affect'ed
advan'tage	affec'tion
advanta'geous	affec'tionate
advanta'ge- ously	affec'tionately
adventi'tious	affida'vit
adven'ture	affil'iate
adven'turer	affil'iated
adven'turess	affilia'tion
ad'verb	affirm'
ad'versary	affirm'ative
ad'verse	affirmed'
ad'versely	affirm'ing
adver'sity	{affix', v.
ad'vertise	{af'fix, n.
ad'vertised	affixed'
adver'tise- ment	affix'ing
	afflict'
ad'vertiser	afflict'ed
ad'vertising	afflict'ing
advice'	afflic'tion
advisabil'ity	af'fluently
advis'able	afford'
advise'	afford'ed
advised'	afford'ing
advis'edly	afforesta'tion
advis'er	affront'
advis'ing	affront'ed
advis'ory	afloat'
ad'vocacy	afore'said
ad'vocate, n.	afraid'
ad'vocate, v.	afresh'
ad'vocated	Af'rican
ae'rial	Afrikaans'
aerobat'ics	Afrikan'der
aer'obus	aft'er
aer'odrome	aft'ermath
aer'ofoil	afternoon'
aeronau'tic	aft'erwards
aer'oplane	again'
aesthet'ic	against'
aesthet'ics	age
affabil'ity	a'ged
af'fable	a'gency
af'fably	agen'da
affair'	a'gent

aggrand'ize-	ail'ment
ment	aim
ag'gravate	aimed
ag'gravated	aim'ing
ag'gravating	aim'less
aggrava'tion	aim'lessly
ag'gregate	aim'lessness
ag'gregated	air
ag'gregating	air'borne
aggrega'tion	air'craft
aggres'sion	air'field
aggress'ive	air'force
aggress'or	air'-hole
aggrieve'	air'-lift
aggrieved'	air'line
aghast'	air'mail
ag'ile	air'minded
agil'ity	air'plane
ag'itate	air'port
ag'itated	air-shaft
ag'itating	air'ship
agita'tion	air'strip
ag'itator	air'tight
	air'way
agnos'tic	air'worthi'ness
ago'	air'worthy
ag'onizing	aisle
ag'ony	akin'
agree'	à la carte'
agree'able	alac'rity
agreed'	alarm'
agree'ing	alarmed'
agree'ment	alarm'ing
agricul'tural	alarm'ingly
	alas'
ag'riculture	al'bum
agricul'turist	al'cohol
aground'	alcohol'ic
a'gue	al'derman
ah	ale
ahead'	alert'
aid	alert'ness
aid'ed	al'gebra
aide-mém'oire	a'lias
aid'ing	al'ibi
ail	a'lien
ailed	a'lienate
ail'ing	a'lienated

a'lienating	
aliena'tion	
alight'	
alight'ed	
alight'ing	
align', aline'	
align'ment	
alike'	
aliment'ary	
al'imony	
alive'	
al'kali	
al'kaline	
all	
allay'	
allayed'	
allay'ing	
allega'tion	
allege'	
alleged'	
alle'giance	
alleg'ing	
all'ergy	
alle'viate	
alle'viated	
alle'viating	
allevia'tion	
al'ley	
al'leyway	
alli'ance	
al'lied	
al'lies	
al'locate	
al'located	
al'locating	
alloca'tion	
allot'	
allot'ment	
allot'ropism	
allot'ted	
allot'ting	
allow'	
allow'able	
allow'ance	
allowed'	
allow'ing	
alloy'	
allude'	

allud'ed	
allud'ing	
allure'	
allur'ing	
allur'ingly	
allu'sion	
allu'via	
al'ly	
al'manac	
almight'y	
a'lmond	
al'most	
aloft'	
alone'	
along'	
along'side	
aloof'	
aloud'	
al'phabet	
alphabet'ic	
alphabet'ical	
Alp'ine	
already'	
al'so	
al'tar	
al'ter	
altera'tion	
alterca'tion	
al'tered	
al'tering	
al'ternate, *v.*	
altern'ate, *a.*	
al'ternated	
altern'ately	
al'ternating	
altern'ative	
altern'atively	
al'ternator	
although'	
al'titude	
altogeth'er	
al'truism	
altruis'tic	
alumin'ium	
alu'minum	
al'ways	
am	
amal'gamate	

amal′gamated	among′
amal′gamating	amongst′
amalgama′tion	amo′ral
amanuen′sis	amoral′ity
amass′	amortiza′tion
amassed′	amor′tize
amass′ing	amor′tizement
am′ateur	amount′
amaze′	amount′ed
amazed′	amount′ing
amaze′ment	amp′
amaz′ing	amper′age
amaz′ingly	amphib′ian
Am′azon	amphithe′atre
ambas′sador	am′ple
am′ber	amplifica′tion
ambigu′ity	am′plified
ambig′uous	am′plifier
ambig′uously	am′plify
ambi′tion	am′plifying
ambi′tious	am′ply
ambi′tiously	am′poule
ambiv′alence	am′putate
ambiv′alent	am′putated
am′bulance	am′putating
am′bush	amputa′tion
ame′liorate	amuse′
ameliora′tion	amused′
amen′	amuse′ment
ame′nable	amus′ing
ame′nably	*an*
amend′	anach′ronism
amend′ed	anae′mia
amend′ment	anaem′ic
amen′ity	anaesthet′ic
Amer′ican	analges′ic
Amer′icanism	anal′ogous
a′miable	anal′ogy
am′icable	an′alyse
am′icably	an′alysed
amid′	an′alysing
amidst′	anal′ysis
amiss′	an′alyst
am′ity	analyt′ic
ammo′nia	analyt′ical
ammuni′tion	an′archist
amoe′bic	an′archy
amok′	anath′ema

anatom'ical	an'notate
anat'omy	an'notated
an'cestor	an'notating
ances'tral	annota'tion
anch'or	announce'
anch'ored	announced'
anch'oring	announce'-
an'cient	ment
and	announc'er
an'ecdote	announc'ing
ane'mic	annoy'
anae'mic	annoy'ance
anesthet'ic	annoyed'
anaesthet'ic	annoy'ing
anew'	an'nual
an'gel	an'nually
angel'ic	annu'ity
an'ger	annul'
an'gered	annul'ling
an'gle	an'num
Ang'lophil	anom'alous
Ang'lophile	anom'aly
Ang'lophobe	anonym'ity
ango'ra	anon'ymous
an'grily	
an'gry	anon'ymously
an'guish	
an'gular	anoph'eles
angular'ity	anoth'er
an'iline	an'swer
an'imal	an'swerable
an'imate	an'swered
an'imated	an'swering
an'imating	
anima'tion	antag'onism
animos'ity	antag'onist
an'iseed	
an'kle	antagonist'ic
an'nals	antag'onize
annex'	
annexa'tion	Antarc'tic
annexed'	antece'dent
annex'ing	an'tedate
anni'hilate	an'tedated
anni'hilated	antenat'al
annihi'lating	an'them
annihila'tion	anthol'ogist
anniver'sary	anthol'ogy
	an'thracite
	an'thrax

anti-air′craft		appalled′	
antibiot′ic		appall′ing	
an′tic		appara′tus	
antic′ipate		appar′el	
antic′ipated		appa′rent	
antic′ipating		appa′rently	
anticipa′tion		appeal′	
an′tidote		appealed′	
antihist′amine		appeal′ing	
an′tiquated		appear′	
antique′		appear′ance	
antiq′uity		appeared′	
anti-semit′ic		appear′ing	
antisep′tic		appease′	
antith′esis		appel′lant	
anti-vivisec′tion		appel′late	
ant′ler		appella′tion	
an′vil		append′	
anxi′ety		append′age	
anx′ious		append′ed	
anx′iously		appen′dices	
an′y		appendici′tis	
an′ybody		append′ing	
an′yhow		appen′dix	
an′yone		appen′dixes	
an′ything		appertain′	
an′ytime		appertained′	
an′yway		appertain′ing	
an′ywhere		ap′petite	
apart′		ap′petize	
apart′heid		ap′petizing	
apart′ment		applaud′	
apathet′ic		applaud′ed	
ap′athy		applaud′ing	
ape′ritif		applause′	
ap′erture		ap′ple	
a′pex		appli′ance	
aph′orism		ap′plicable	
aphrodis′iac		ap′plicant	
apiece′		applica′tion	
apologet′ic		applied′	
apolo′gia		apply′	
apol′ogize		apply′ing	
apol′ogized		appoint′	
apol′ogizing		appoint′ed	
apol′ogy		appoint′ing	
apos′tle		appoint′ment	
appal′			

appor'tion	A'pril
appor'tioned	a'pron
appor'tioning	apropos'
appor'tion-ment	apt
	apt'itude
ap'posite	apt'ly
apprais'al	apt'ness
appraise'	a'qualung
appraised'	aquamarine'
appre'ciable	a'qua-planing
appre'ciate	aqua'rium
appre'ciated	aquat'ic
appre'ciating	a'queduct
apprecia'tion	Ar'ab
appre'ciative	Ara'bian
apprehend'	Ar'abic
apprehend'ed	ar'able
apprehend'ing	ar'biter
apprehen'sion	arb'itrage
apprehen'sive	ar'bitrarily
appren'tice	ar'bitrary
appren'ticed	ar'bitrate
appren'tice-ship	ar'bitrated
	ar'bitrating
approach'	arbitra'tion
approach'able	ar'bitrator
approached'	arbor'eal
approach'ing	ar'bour, ar'bor
approba'tion	arc
appro'priate	arcade'
appro'priated	arch
appro'priately	archa'ic
appro'priate-ness	archbish'op
	ar'chitect
appro'priating	
appropria'tion	architect'ural
approv'al	
approve'	ar'chitecture
approved'	
approv'ing	Arc'tic
approv'ingly	ar'dent
approx'imate	ar'dently
approx'imated	ar'dour, ar'dor
approx'imately	ar'duous
approx'imat-ing	*are*
	a'rea
approxima'-tion	are'na
	Ar'gentine
	ar'gosy

ar'gue	
ar'gued	
ar'guing	
ar'gument	
argumen'ta-	
tive	
ar'id	
arid'ity	
aright'	
arise'	
aris'en	
aris'ing	
aristoc'racy	
ar'istocrat	
aristocrat'ic	
arith'metic	
arithmet'ical	
arm	
Armagedd'on	
ar'mament	
ar'mature	
arm'chair	
armed	
arm'ing	
arm'istice	
ar'mour,	
ar'mor	
arms	
ar'my	
aro'ma	
arose'	
around'	
arouse'	
aroused'	
arous'ing	
arraign'	
arraigned'	
arrange'	
arranged'	
arrange'ment	
arrang'ing	
array'	
arrayed'	
arrear'	
arrears'	
arrest'	

arrest'ed	
arrest'ing	
arri'val	
arrive'	
arrived'	
arriv'ing	
ar'rogance	
ar'rogant	
ar'rogantly	
ar'row	
ar'senal	
ar'senic	
ar'son	
art	
ar'tery	
arte'sian	
art'ful	
ar'ticle	
art'ifact	
art'ifice	
artifi'cial	
artil'lery	
ar'tisan	
art'ist	
artist'ic	
ar'tistry	
art'less	
as	
asbes'tos	
ascend'	
ascen'dancy	
ascend'ency	
ascertain'	
ascertained'	
ascet'ic	
ascor'bic	
ascribe'	
ascribed'	
ascrib'ing	
ash	
ashamed'	
ashore'	
A'sian	
Asiat'ic	
aside'	
asinin'ity	
ask	
askance'	

asked		assign'	
asleep'		assigned'	
as'pect		assignee'	
asper'sion		assign'ment	
as'phalt		assignor'	
asphyxia'tion		assigns'	
aspi'rant		assim'ilate	
as'pirate, n.		assim'ilated	
as'pirate, v.		assim'ilating	
aspira'tion		assimila'tion	
aspire'		assort'	
aspired'		assist'	
aspir'in		assist'ance	
aspir'ing		assist'ant	
assail'		assist'ed	
assail'ant		assist'ing	
assailed'		assize'	
assail'ing		assiz'es	
assas'sin		asso'ciate	
assas'sinate		asso'ciated	
assas'sinated		asso'ciating	
assault'		associa'tion	
assault'ed		assort'	
assault'ing		assort'ed	
assay'		assort'ing	
assayed'		assort'ment	
assay'er		assuage'	
assay'ing		assume'	
assem'ble		assumed'	
assem'bled		assum'ing	
assem'bling		assump'tion	
assem'bly		assur'ance	
assent'		assure'	
assent'ed		assured'	
assent'ing		assur'edly	
assert'		assur'ing	
assert'ed		as'ter	
assert'ing		as'terisk	
asser'tion		asth'ma	
assess'		astir'	
assessed'		aston'ish	
assess'ing		aston'ished	
assess'ment		aston'ishing	
assess'or		aston'ishment	
as'sets		astound'	
assidu'ity		astound'ed	
assid'uous		astrakhan'	
assid'uously			

astray'
astrin'gent
as'trodome
astrol'ogy
as'tronaut
astronaut'ics
astron'omer
astron'omy
astute'
asun'der
asy'lum
at
ate
a'theist
ath'lete
athlet'ic
athlet'ics
Atlan'tic
At'las, at'las
at'mosphere
atmospher'ic
atmosphe'rics
at'om
at'omizer
aton'al
atone'
atoned'
atone'ment
atro'cious
atro'ciously
atroc'ity
at'rophy
attach'
attached'
attach'ing
attach'ment
attack'
attacked'
attack'ing
attain'
attain'able
attained'
attain'ing
attain'ment
attempt'
attempt'ed
attempt'ing
attend'

attend'ance
attend'ant
attend'ed
attend'ing
atten'tion
atten'tive
atten'tively
atten'uate
attest'
attesta'tion
attest'ed
attest'er,
  attest'or
attest'ing
at'tic
attire'
attired'
at'titude
attor'ney
Attor'ney-
  Gen'eral
attract'
attract'ed
attract'ing
attrac'tion
attract'ive
attract'ively
attrib'utable
{at'tribute, n.
{attrib'ute, v.
attrib'uted
attrib'uting
au'burn
auc'tion
auc'tioneer'
auda'cious
auda'ciously
audac'ity
audibil'ity
au'dible
au'dience
au'dio
au'dit
au'dited
au'diting
au'ditor
audito'rium
aught

augment'	
augment'ed	
augment'ing	
au'gur	
au'gured	
{Au'gust, *n.*	
{august', *adj.*	
aunt	
au'ral	
au'spices	
auspi'cious	
auspi'ciously	
Australa'sian	
Austra'lian	
Aus'trian	
aut'archy	
authen'tic	
authen'ticate	
authen'ticated	
authentic'ity	
au'thor	
au'thoress	
authoritar'ian	
authori-	
tar'ianism	
author'itative	
author'ita-	
tively	
author'ity	
authoriza'tion	
au'thorize	
au'thorized	
au'thorizing	
au'thorship	
aut'o	
autobiograph'-	
ical	
autobiog'raphy	
autoc'racy	
au'tocrat	
autocrat'ic	
au'tograph	
aut'omate	
automat'ic	
automa'tion	
autom'aton	
automobile'	

automot'ive	
auto-sugges'tion	
au'tumn	
autum'nal	
auxil'iary	
avail'	
avail'able	
availed'	
avail'ing	
av'alanche	
av'arice	
avari'cious	
avenge'	
avenged'	
av'enue	
aver'	
av'erage	
av'eraged	
av'eraging	
averse'	
aver'sion	
avert'	
avert'ed	
avert'ing	
avia'tion	
a'viator	
a'viatrix	
av'id	
av'idly	
avoca'do	
avoca'tion	
avoid'	
avoid'able	
avoid'ance	
avoid'ed	
avoid'ing	
avoirdupois'	
avow'	
avow'al	
await'	
await'ed	
await'ing	
awake'	
awa'ken	
awa'kened	
awa'kening	
award'	
award'ed	

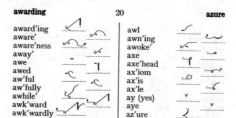

award'ing	awl
aware'	awn'ing
aware'ness	awoke'
away'	axe
awe	axe'head
awed	ax'iom
aw'ful	ax'is
aw'fully	ax'le
awhile'	ay (yes)
awk'ward	aye
awk'wardly	az'ure

B

bab'ble
ba'by
bab'y-sitt'er
bach'elor
bacil'lus
back
back'ben'cher
back'bone
back'chat
back'cloth
back'fire
back'ground
back'log
back'marker
back'num'ber
back'scratch'er
back'wards
ba'con
bacte'ria
bacteriol'ogist
bad
bade
badge
bad'ly
baf'fle
baf'fled
baf'fling
bag
bag'gage
bag'pipe
bail
bailed
bai'liff
bait
bait'ing
bake
bak'er
bak'ery
bak'ing
bal'ance

bal'anced
bal'ance-sheet
bal'ancing
bal'cony
bald
bald'headed
bald'ly
bale
baled
balk
ball
bal'lad
bal'last
ballerin'a
balletomane'
balletoma'nia
balloon'
bal'lot
bal'loted
ballyhoo'
balm'y
bal'sa
bamboo'
ban
bana'na
band
band'age
band'aging
band'ed
band'master
band'saw
band'wag'on
bang
banged
ban'ish
ban'ished
ban'ishment
bank
bank'book
banked

21

bank′er	bar′tered
bank′ing	bar′tering
bank′rupt	bas′cule
bank′ruptcy	base
ban′ner	base′ball
ban′quet	based
ban′ter	base′less
bap′tism	base′ment
Bap′tist	bash′ful
baptize′	ba′sic
baptized′	bas′ically
bar	ba′sin
	ba′sing
barathe′a	ba′sis
barbar′ic	bas′ket
bar′barous	bas′ketball
bar′ber	bat
barb′itone	batch
barbiturate′	bath
bare	bathe
bared	bath′er
bare′faced	bath′ing
bare′ly	bath′room
bar′est	bath′yscaphe
	bath′ysphere
bar′gain	bat′tery
bar′gaining	bat′tle
barge	bat′tleship
bar′ing	baulk
bark	baux′ite
	Bava′rian
bark′ing	bay
bar′ley	bazaar′
barn	*be*
barom′eter	beach
baromet′ric	beach′-
	comber
baroque′	bea′con
bar′rage	bead
barred	beak
bar′rel	beam
bar′ren	beamed
barricade′	bean
barrica′ded	bean′o
barrica′ding	bear
bar′rier	bear′able
bar′ring	beard
bar′row	beard′ed
bar′ter	

bear'er	befriend'ed
bear'ing	befriend'ing
beast	beg
beast'ly	began
beat	beg'gar
beat'en	beg'ging
beat'ing	begin'
beau'tified	begin'ner
beau'tiful	begin'ning
beau'tify	begrudge'
beau'tifying	begrudg'ing
beau'ty	beguile'
bea'ver	beguiled'
became'	begun'
because'	behalf'
beck'on	behave'
beck'oned	beha'ving
beck'oning	behav'iour,
become'	behav'ior
becom'ing	behav'iourism
bed	behav'iourist
bed'ding	beheld'
bed'pan	behind'
bedrag'gle	behold'
bedrag'gled	behoove'
bed'rock	beige
bed'room	*be'ing*
bed'sit'ter	belat'ed
bed'spread	bel'fry
bed'stead	Bel'gian
bed'time	**belief'**
bee	believ'able
beech	believe'
beef	believed'
bee'hive	believ'er
been	believ'ing
beer	belit'tle
beet	belit'tled
beet'le	bell
befall'	bellig'erent
befal'len	bel'low
befell'	bel'lowing
befit	bell'push
befit'ted	belong
befit'ting	belonged'
before'	belong'ing
*before'*hand	beloved'
befriend'	belov'ed

below'	
belt	
bench	
bend	
bend'able	
bend'ing	
beneath'	
benedic'tion	
benefac'tor	
ben'efice	
benef'icence	
benef'icent	
benef'icently	
benefi'cial	
benefi'ciary	
ben'efit	
ben'efited	
ben'efiting	
benev'olence	
benev'olent	
benign'	
benig'nant	
benign'ly	
bent	
ben'zine	
bequeath'	
bequeathed'	
bequeath'ing	
bequest'	
bereave'	
bereaved'	
bereave'ment	
bereft'	
ber'et	
ber'ry	
ber'serk	
berth	
beseech'	
beseech'ing	
beset'	
beset'ting	
beside'	
besides'	
besiege'	
besieg'ing	

best	
bestow'	
bestowed'	
bet	
bête-noire	
betray'	
betray'al	
betroth'	
betroth'al	
betrothed'	
bet'ter	
bet'tering	
bet'terment	
bet'ting	
between'	
betwixt'	
bev'el	
bev'elled, bev'eled	
bev'erage	
beware'	
bewil'der	
bewil'dered	
bewil'dering	
bewil'derment	
beyond'	
bian'nual	
bi'as	
bi'ased	
Bi'ble	
Bib'lical	
bibliog'raphy	
bi'cycle	
bid	
bid'der	
bid'ding	
bien'nial	
bifo'cal	
bifo'cals	
big	
big'amist	
big'amous	
big'amy	
big'ger	
big'gest	
big'ot	
big'oted	
big'otry	

bikin'i	bit'ten
	bit'ter
biling'ualism	bit'terness
bil'ious	bitu'minous
bil'iousness	bizarre'
bill	black
billed	black'berry
bil'let	black'bird
bill'iards	black'board
bil'lion	black'en
bil'low	black'ened
bimet'allism,	black'ening
bimet'alism	black'guard
bind	black'mail
bind'er	black'smith
bind'ery	blad'der
bind'ing	blade
bing'o	blame
binoc'ular	blamed
	blame'less
biochem'ical	blame'worthy
biochem'ist	blank
biochem'istry	blank'et
biog'rapher	blaspheme'
biograph'ic	blasphemed'
biograph'ical	blas'phemous
biog'raphy	blas'phemy
biolog'ical	blast
biol'ogy	blast'ed
birch	blast'ing
bird	bla'tant
bird's'-eye	blaze
birth	blazed
birth'-control'	blaz'er
birth'day	bleach
birth'mark	bleach'ing
birth'place	bleak
birth'rate	bled
birth'right	bleed
bis'cuit	bleed'ing
bisect'	blem'ish
bisect'ed	blend
bisect'ing	blend'ed
bish'op	bless
bis'muth	blessed
bit	bless'ed
bite	bless'ing
bit'ing	blest

blew		
blight		
blight'ed		
blight'ing		
blind		
blind'ed		
blind'fold		
blind'folded		
blind'ing		
blind'ly		
blind'ness		
blindspot		
blink'ered		
bliss		
bliss'ful		
bliss'fulness		
blis'ter		
blis'tered		
blis'tering		
blithe		
blitz		
bliz'zard		
block		
blockade'		
blockad'ed		
blockad'ing		
blocked		
block'head		
blond, blonde		
blood		
blood'-group		
blood'shed		
bloom		
bloomed		
blos'som		
blos'somed		
blot		
blotch		
blot'ter		
blouse		
blow		
blow'ing		
blow'lamp		
blown		
blue		
blue'berry		
blue'-chip		
bluff		

blun'der		
blun'dered		
blun'dering		
blunt		
blunt'ed		
blunt'ly		
blur		
blurred		
blur'ring		
blurt		
blurt'ed		
blush		
blushed		
blush'ing		
blus'ter		
blus'tered		
blus'tering		
blus'tery		
board		
board'ed		
board'er		
board'ing		
board'ing-house		
boast		
boast'ed		
boast'ful		
boast'fulness		
boast'ing		
boat		
boat'house		
boat'swain		
bob		
bobbed		
bob'sleigh		
bod'ily		
bod'y		
bod'yguard		
boff'in		
bo'gus		
Bohe'mian		
boil		
boiled		
boil'er		
bois'terous		
bois'terously		
bold		
bold'er		

bold'ly	bored
bold'ness	bore'dom
Bol'shevik	bo'ring
bol'ster	born
bol'stered	borne
bol'stering	bor'ough
bolt	bor'row
bolt'ed	bor'rowed
bomb	bor'rower
bom'bard, n.	bor'rowing
bombard', v.	bos'om
bombard'ed	boss
bombard'ing	bot'anist
bombard'ment	bot'any
bombast'ic	both
bomb'proof	both'er
bomb'shell	both'ered
bond	both'ering
bond'age	bot'tle
bond'ed	bot'tleneck
bond'holder	bot'tling
bone	bot'tom
bon'fire	boudoir'
bon'net	bough
bo'nus	bought
book	boul'der
book'binder	boul'evard
book'binding	bounce
book'case	bounced
book'-keeper	bounc'ing
book'-keeping	bound
book'let	bound'ary
book'seller	bound'ed
book'shelf	bound'ing
book'stall	bound'less
book'store	boun'tiful
book'worm	boun'ty
boom	bouquet'
boomed	bourgeois'
boon	bour'geois
boost	bout
boost'er	boutique'
boot	bow (part of
booth	violin; a
bor'der	weapon)
bor'dering	bow (part of a
bor'derline	ship; to bend
bore	the body)

bowed	
bow'els	
bow'er	
bow'ing	
bowl	
bowled	
bowl'er	
bow'line	
box	
boxed	
box'er	
box'-office	
boy	
boy'cott	
boy'hood	
boy'ish	
boy'ishly	
bra	
brace	
braced	
brace'let	
bra'ces	
brack'et	
brack'eted	
brag	
bragged	
braid	
braid'ed	
braid'ing	
Braille	
brain	
brain'less	
brain'wash	
brain'wave	
brake	
branch	
branch'ing	
brand	
brand'ed	
bran'dish	
bran'dished	
bran'dy	
brass	
brass'erie	
brass'ière	
brava'do	
brave	
brave'ly	

brav'ery	
brav'est	
brawl	
brawled	
brawn	
bra'zen	
Brazil'ian	
breach	
bread	
breadth	
bread'winner	
break	
break'able	
break'age	
break'down	
break'fast	
break'ing	
break'neck	
break'water	
breast	
breath	
breathe	
breath'less	
bred	
breech	
breed	
breed'er	
breed'ing	
breeze	
breez'y	
breth'ren	
brev'ity	
brew	
brew'ing	
bribe	
bribed	
brib'ery	
brick	
brick'layer	
brick'work	
brick'yard	
bri'dal	
bride	
bridge	
bri'dle	
bri'dled	
brief	
brief'est	

brief'ly
brigade'
brigadier'
brig'and
bright
bright'en
bright'er
bright'ly
bright'ness
bril'liance
bril'liancy
bril'liant
bril'liantly
brim
brim'ful
brine
bring
brink
brisk
bris'tle
bris'tled
Britan'nic
Brit'ish
brit'tle
brit'tleness
broach
broach'ing
broad
broad'cast
broad'caster
broad'casting
broad'en
broad'er
broad'ly
broad'mind'ed
brocade'
brocad'ed
bro'chure
brogue
broke
bro'ken
brok'en-
  heart'ed
bro'ker
bro'mide
bron'chial
bronchi'tis
bronze

bronzed
bronz'ing
brooch
brood
brood'ed
brood'ing
brook
broom
broth
broth'er
broth'erhood
broth'er-in-law
brought
brow
brown
bruise
bruised
brunette'
brunt
brush
brushed
brush'wood
brusque
bru'tal
brutal'ity
bru'tally
brute
bub'ble
bub'bled
buck
buck'et
buc'kle
buck'ram
buck'wheat
bucol'ic
bud
bud'ding
budg'erigar'
budg'et
budg'eting
buff
buf'falo
buf'fet
buf'feted
bug'bear
bug'gy
bu'gle
bu'gler

build	burg'lary
build'er	bur'ial
build'ing	bur'ied
built	burlesque'
bulb	bur'ly
bulge	burn
bulk	burned
bulk'y	burn'er
bull	burn'ing
bull'doze	burnt
bull'dozer	bur'row
bul'let	bur'rowed
bul'letin	bur'rowing
bul'let-proof	burst
bul'lied	burst'ing
bul'lion	bur'y
bul'lock	bur'ying
bul'ly	bus
bul'lying	bush
bul'wark	bush'el
bump	bus'ier
bumped	bus'iest
bump'er	bus'ily
bump'ing	bus'iness
bump'tious	bus'inesslike
bump'tious-	bus'inessman'
ness	bust
bun	bus'tle
bunch	bus'tled
bun'dle	bus'y
bun'galow	*but*
bun'gle	butch'er
bunk	but'ler
bunk'er	butt
buoy	butt'ed
buoy'ancy	but'ter
buoy'ant	but'ton
buoy'antly	but'tonhole
buoyed	buy
bur'den	buy'er
	buy'ing
bur'densome	buzz
	by, bye
bureau'	by'pass
bur'eaucrat	by'-prod'uct
bureaucrat'ic	by'stander
burg	by'word
burg'lar	

C

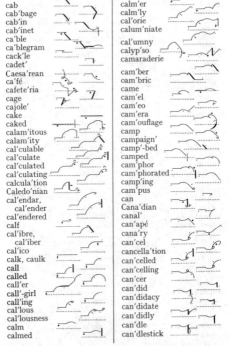

cab
cab'bage
cab'in
cab'inet
ca'ble
ca'blegram
cack'le
cadet'
Caesa'rean
ca'fé
cafete'ria
cage
cajole'
cake
caked
calam'itous
calam'ity
cal'culable
cal'culate
cal'culated
cal'culating
calcula'tion
Caledo'nian
cal'endar,
  cal'ender
cal'endered
calf
cal'ibre,
  cal'iber
cal'ico
calk, caulk
call
called
call'er
call'-girl
call'ing
cal'lous
cal'lousness
calm
calmed

calm'er
calm'ly
cal'orie
calum'niate
cal'umny
calyp'so
camaraderie
cam'ber
cam'bric
came
cam'el
cam'eo
cam'era
cam'ouflage
camp
campaign'
camp'-bed
camped
cam'phor
cam'phorated
camp'ing
cam'pus
can
Cana'dian
canal'
can'apé
cana'ry
can'cel
cancella'tion
can'celled
can'celling
can'cer
can'did
can'didacy
can'didate
can'didly
can'dle
can'dlestick

can'dour,	
can'dor	
can'dy	
cane	
can'ine	*or*
can'ister	
can'ker	
can'kered	
canned	
can'nery	
can'ning	
can'non	
can'not	
canoe'	
can'on	
cañ'on	
can'opy	
cant	
cantan'kerous	
canteen'	
can'ter	
can'tered	
can'ton	
can'vas,	
adj., n.	
can'vass, *v.*	
can'vassed	
can'vasser	
can'yon	
cap	
capabil'ity	
ca'pable	
ca'pably	
capa'cious	
capac'itance	
capac'itor	
capac'ity	
cape	
cap'ital	
cap'italism	
cap'italist	
capitalis'tic	
capitaliza'tion	
cap'italize	
Cap'itol	
capit'ulate	
capitula'tion	
caprice'	

capri'cious	
capsize'	
capsized'	
cap'stan	
cap'sule	
cap'tain	
cap'tion	
cap'tivate	
cap'tivated	
captiva'tion	
cap'tive	
captiv'ity	
cap'tor	
cap'ture	
cap'tured	
car	
car'amel	
car'at	
car'avan	
car'bide	
carbohy'drate	
carbol'ic	
car'bon	
carbon'ic	
car'bonizer	
car'burate	
car'burettor,	
car'buretter	
car'cass	
carcinogen'ic	
card	
card'board	
car'diac	
car'digan	
car'dinal	
card'-in'dex	
car'diogram	
car'diograph	
care	
cared	
career'	
career'ist	
care'free	
care'ful	
care'fully	
care'less	
care'lessness	
caress'	

caressed'		cas'tigate	
car'et		castiga'tion	
care'worn		cast'ing	
car'go		cast'-iron	
car'icature		cas'tle	
car'icatured		cas'tor	
car'ing		cas'tor oil	
car'mine		cas'ual	
carna'tion		cas'ualism	
car'nival		cas'ually	
car'nivore		cas'uals	
carniv'orous		cas'ualty	
car'ol		cat	
carp		cat'aclysm	
car'penter		cat'alogue	
car'pentry		cat'apult	
car'pet		cat'aract	
car'riage		catarrh'	
car'ried		catarrh'al	
car'rier		catas'trophe	
car'rot		catastroph'ic	
car'ry		catch	
car'rying		catch'-phrase	
cart		catch'ing	
cart'age		cat'echism	
carte blanche'		categor'ical	
cart'ed		cat'egory	
car'ton		ca'ter	
cartoon'		ca'tering	
cartoon'ist		cat'erpillar	
car'tridge		cathe'dral	
carve		Cath'olic,	
carved		cath'olic	
carv'er		Cathol'icism	
carv'ing		cat'tle	
cascade'		caught	
case		caul'dron	
cash		cau'liflower	
cashed		caulk	
cashier'		cause	
cash'ing		caused	
cash'mere		caus'ing	
cash'-register		caus'tic	
cask		cau'terize	
cas'ket		cau'tion	
cassette		cau'tionary	
cast		cau'tioned	
caste		cau'tioning	

cau'tious	cen'tigrade
cau'tiously	cen'tral
cavalcade	centraliza'tion
cavalier'	cen'tralize
cav'alry	cen'tralized
cave	cen'tre
cav'ern	cen'tred
cav'il	cen'tring
cav'ity	cen'tury
cease	ceram'ics
ceased	ce'real
cease'less	ceremo'nial
cease'lessly	ceremo'nious
ceas'ing	cer'emony
ce'dar	cer'tain
cede	cer'tainly
ce'ded	cer'tainty
ceil'ing	cert'ifiable
cel'ebrate	certif'icate
cel'ebrated	certif'icated
cel'ebrating	certifica'tion
celebra'tion	cer'tified
celeb'rity	cer'tify
celer'ity	cessa'tion
cel'ery	chafe
celes'tial	chafed
cel'ibacy	chaff
cel'ibate	cha'fing
cell	chagrin'
cel'lar	chain
cell'ophane	chair
cel'luloid	chair'man
cel'lulose	chair'manship
Celt'ic	chalk
cement'	chal'lenge
cement'ed	chal'lenged
cement'ing	chal'lenger
cem'etery	cham'ber
cen'otaph	cham'berlain
cen'sor	chame'leon
cen'sorship	champagne'
cen'sure	cham'pion
cen'sured	cham'pioned
cen'suring	cham'pionship
cen'sus	chance
cen'suses	chanced
cent	chan'cellor
cen'tenary	chan'cery

change	chat'ted
change'able	chat'tel
changed	chat'ter
chan'ging	chauf'feur
chan'nel	cheap
chant	cheap'en
chant'ed	cheap'ly
cha'os	cheat
chaot'ic	cheat'ed
chap	cheat'ing
chap'el	check
chap'eron	check'ing
chap'lain	check'-up
chap'ter	cheek
char	cheer
	cheered
char'acter	cheer'ful
	cheer'fulness
characterist'ic	cheer'ing
characteris'tic-	cheer'less
ally	cheese
char'coal	chef
charge	chem'ical
charge'able	chem'ist
charged	chem'istry
charg'ing	cheque
char'itable	cheque'-book
char'ity	cher'ish
char'la'dy	cher'ished
char'latan	cher'ry
charm	cher'ub
charm'ing	chess
charred	chest
chart	chest'nut
char'ter	chew
char'tered	chewed
char'woman	chew'ing
cha'ry	chic
chase	chick'en
chased	chic'ory
chasm	chief
chas'sis	chief'ly
chaste	chil'blain
chastise'	child
chastised'	child'hood
chas'tisement	child'ish
chastis'ing	child'ishly
chas'tity	chil'dren
chat	

chill		Christ'mas	
chilled		chromat'ic	
chime		chrome	
chimed		chro'mium	
chim'ney		chrom'osome	
chimpan'zee		chron'ic	
chin		chron'icle	
chi'na		chronolog'-ical	
Chinese'			
chintz		chrysan'the-mum	
chip			
chirop'odist		chum	
chirop'ody		church	
chiroprac'tor		church'yard	
chirp		churl'ish	
chis'el		churl'ishly	
chis'el(l)er		churn	
chiv'alrous		chute	
chiv'alry		chut'ney	
chlor'inate		ci'der	
chlo'roform		cigar'	
choc'olate		cigarette'	
choice		cinch	
choi'cest		cin'der	
choir		cin'e	
choke		cine-cam'era	
chol'era		cin'ema	
choose		cinemat'o-graph	
choos'ing			
chop		cin'namon	
chopped		ci'pher	
chop'per		cir'ca	
chop'ping		cir'cle	
cho'ral		cir'cuit	
chord		cir'cuited	
chore		circu'itous	
choreog'rapher		cir'cular	
choreog'raphy		cir'cularize	
cho'rus		cir'culate	
chose		cir'culated	
chos'en		cir'culating	
Christ		circula'tion	
chris'ten		circum'ference	
Chris'tendom		circumscribe'	
chris'tened		circumscribed'	
Chris'tian		cir'cumspect	
Christian'ity			

circumspec'- tion	clas'sify
cir'cumstance	class'room
cir'cumstanced	clat'ter
circumstan'tial	clause
circumvent'	claustrophob'ia
cir'cus	claw
cis'tern	clawed
cit'adel	clay
cita'tion	clean
cite	cleaned
ci'ted	clean'er
cit'izen	clean'est
cit'izenship	clean'ing
cit'rus	clean'liness
cit'y	clean'ly, *adj.*
civ'ic	clean'ly, *adv.*
civ'il	cleanse
civil'ian	cleans'er
civil'ity	cleans'ing
civiliza'tion	clear
civ'ilize	clear'ance
civ'ilized	cleared
clad	clear'er
claim	clear'est
claim'ant	clear'ing
claimed	
claim'ing	clear'ing-house
clam'ber	
clam'bered	clear'ly
clam'our, clam'or	clear'ness
clam'orous	clear'-sighted
clamp	clear'way
clandes'tine	clem'ency
clang	clench
clanged	clench'ing
clap	cler'gy
clar'ify	cler'gyman
clash	cler'ic
clashed	cler'ical
clasp	clerk
class	clerk'ship
classed	clev'er
clas'sic	clew
clas'sical	cliché
classifica'tion	click
classifi'able	cli'ent
	clientele'
	cliff
	cli'mate

climat′ic	clus′ter
cli′max	clus′tered
climb	clus′tering
climbed	clutch
climb′er	clutch′ing
climb′ing	coach
clinch	coach′ing
cling .	coach′work
cling′ing	coal
clin′ic	coal′face
clinic′ian	coal′-gas
clink	coali′tion
clink′er	coal′-tar
clip	coarse
clipped	coars′en
clip′ping	coarse′ness
clique	coars′est
cloak	coast
clock	coast′al
clock′work	coast′guard
clog	coast′ing
clogged	coast′line
clois′ter	coat
close	coat′ed
closed	coax
close′ly	coax′ial
clos′est	cob′bler
clos′et	co′caine
close′up	cock
clo′sure	co′co
clot	co′coa
cloth	cocoon′
clothe	cod
cloth′ier	code
cloth′ing	cod′icil
cloud	cod′ify
cloud′burst	co′ed′
cloud′ed	coed′ucate
clo′ver	coeduca′tional
clo′verleaf	coerce′
clown	coer′cion
club	cof′fee
club′-house	cof′fer
clue	cof′fin
clump	cog
clum′sily	co′gency
clum′sy	co′gent
clung	co′gently

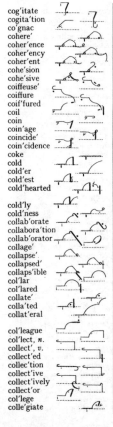

cog'itate
cogita'tion
co'gnac
cohere'
coher'ence
coher'ency
coher'ent
cohe'sion
cohe'sive
coiffeuse'
coiffure
coif'fured
coil
coin
coin'age
coincide'
coin'cidence
coke
cold
cold'er
cold'est
cold'hearted

cold'ly
cold'ness
collab'orate
collabora'tion
collab'orator
collage'
collapse'
collapsed'
collaps'ible
col'lar
col'lared
collate'
colla'ted
collat'eral

col'league
col'lect, *n.*
collect', *v.*
collect'ed
collec'tion
collect'ive
collect'ively
collect'or
col'lege
colle'giate

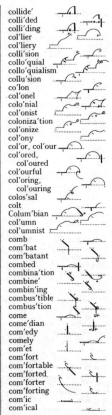

collide'
colli'ded
colli'ding
col'lier
col'liery
colli'sion
collo'quial
collo'quialism
collu'sion
co'lon
col'onel
colo'nial
col'onist
coloniza'tion
col'onize
col'ony
col'or, col'our
col'ored,
  col'oured
col'orful
col'orful
col'oring,
  col'ouring
colos'sal
colt
Colum'bian
col'umn
col'umnist
comb
com'bat
com'batant
combed
combina'tion
combine'
combin'ing
combus'tible
combus'tion
come
come'dian
com'edy
comely
com'et
com'fort
com'fortable
com'forted
com'forter
com'forting
com'ic
com'ical

com'ing	commo'tion
command'	com'mune, *n.*
command'ed	commune', *v.*
command'er	commu'nicate
command'- ment	commu'ni- cated
commem'orate	communica'- tion
commem'- orated	commun'ion
commemora'- tion	commu'niqué
commence'	com'munism
commenced'	com'munist
commence'- ment	commu'nity
commend'	commuta'tion
commend'able	commute'
commenda'- tion	com'pact, *n.*
commen'- datory	compact', *v.,adj.*
commend'ed	compan'ion
commen'surate	compan'ion- ship
com'ment	com'pany
com'mentary	com'parable
com'mented	compar'ative
com'merce	compar'atively
commer'cial	compare'
commer'cialize	compared'
commer'cially	compar'ing
commissar'	compar'ison
commissa'riat	compart'ment
commis'sion	com'pass
commis'sioner	compas'sion
commit'	compas'sionate
commit'ment	compatibil'ity
commit'ted	compat'ible
commit'tee	compat'riot
commit'ting	compel'
commo'dious	compelled'
commod'ity	compen'dium
com'mon	com'pensate
com'moner	com'pensated
com'monest	com'pensating
com'monly	compensa'tion
com'monplace	compete'
com'mon- wealth	compet'ed
	com'petence
	com'petent
	com'petently
	compet'ing

competi'tion
compet'itive
compet'itor
compila'tion
compile'
compiled'
compi'ler
compla'cency
compla'cent
compla'cently
complain'
complain'ant
complained'
complain'ing
complaint'
complais'ant
com'plement
complement'-
ary
complete'
comple'ted
complete'ly
complete'ness
complet'ing
comple'tion
com'plex
complex'ion
complex'ity
compli'ance
compli'ant
com'plicate
com'plicated
complica'tion
complic'ity
complied'
com'pliment
compliment'-
ary
com'plimented
comply'
comply'ing
compo'nent
compose'
composed'
compo'ser
com'posite
composi'tion
compos'itor

compo'sure
com'pound,
  n.
compound',
  v.
compound'ed
comprehend'
comprehend'ed
comprehend'-
  ing
comprehen'-
  sible
comprehen'-
  sion
comprehen'-
  sive
com'press, n.
compress', v.
compressed'
compres'sion
comprise'
comprised'
com'promise
com'promised
comptrol'ler
compul'sion
compul'sorily
compul'sory
compunc'tion
computa'tion
compute'
compu'ter
com'rade
con'cave
conceal'
concealed'
conceal'ment
concede'
conce'ded
conceit'
conceit'ed
conceiv'able
conceive'
conceived'
con'centrate
con'centrated
con'centrating
concentra'tion

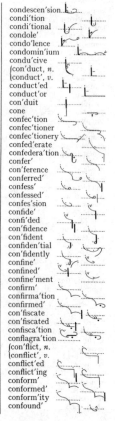

concep'tion	
concern'	
concerned'	
concern'ing	
con'cert, n.	
concert', v.	
concer'to	
conces'sion	
concession(n)aire'	
concil'iate	
concil'iated	
concilia'tion	
concise'	
concise'ly	
concise'ness	
conclude'	
conclu'ded	
conclu'ding	
conclu'sion	
conclu'sive	
conclu'sively	
concoct'	
concoct'ed	
concoct'ing	
concoc'tion	
concom'itant	
con'cord	
con'course	
con'crete	
concur'	
concurred'	
concur'rence	
concur'rent	
concur'rently	
concus'sion	
condemn'	
condemna'tion	
condemned'	
condemn'ing	
condensa'tion	
condense'	
condensed'	
condens'er	
condens'ing	
condescend'	
condescend'ed	
condescend'ing	

condescen'sion	
condi'tion	
condi'tional	
condole'	
condo'lence	
condomin'ium	
condu'cive	
con'duct, n.	
conduct', v.	
conduct'ed	
conduct'or	
con'duit	
cone	
confec'tion	
confec'tioner	
confec'tionery	
confed'erate	
confedera'tion	
confer'	
con'ference	
conferred'	
confess'	
confessed'	
confes'sion	
confide'	
confi'ded	
con'fidence	
con'fident	
confiden'tial	
con'fidently	
confine'	
confined'	
confine'ment	
confirm'	
confirma'tion	
confirmed'	
con'fiscate	
con'fiscated	
confisca'tion	
conflagra'tion	
con'flict, n.	
conflict', v.	
conflict'ed	
conflict'ing	
conform'	
conformed'	
conform'ity	
confound'	

confound'ed
confront'
confront'ed
confront'ing
confuse'
confused'
confu'sion
congeal'
conge'nial
congen'ially
congen'ital
conges'tion
conglomera'-
  tion
congrat'ulate
congrat'ulated
congratula'tion
con'gregate
con'gregated
con'gregating
congrega'tion
congrega'-
  tional
con'gress
congres'sional
con'gressmen
conjec'ture
conjec'tured
con'jugal
conjunc'tion
conjure'
con'jure
conjured'
con'jured
con'jurer
connect'
connect'ed
connec'tion,
  connex'ion
conni'vance
connive'
con'quer
con'quered
con'queror
con'quest
con'science
conscien'tious

conscien'-
  tiously
con'scious
con'sciously
con'sciousness
con'script,
  adj.
conscript', v.
conscrip'tion
con'secrate
con'secrated
consecra'tion
consec'utive
consec'utively
consen'sus
consent'
consent'ed
con'sequence
con'sequent
con'sequently
conserva'tion
conserv'ative
conserv'atively
conserve'
consid'er
consid'erable
consid'erably
consid'erate
consid'erately
considera'tion
consid'ered
consid'ering
consign'
consigned'
consignee'
consign'er
consign'ment
consignor'
consist'
consist'ed
consist'ency
consist'ent
consist'ently
consist'ing
consola'tion
console'
consoled'
consol'idate

consol'idated
consol'idating
consolida'tion
con'sonant
consonan'tal
con'sort, *n.*
consort', *v.*
consort'ed
consor'tium
conspic'uous
conspic'uously
conspir'acy
conspir'ator
conspire'
conspired'
con'stable
constab'ulary
con'stant
con'stantly
consterna'tion
constit'uency
constit'uent
con'stitute
con'stituted
con'stituting
constitu'tion
constitu'tional
constitu'tion-
  ally
constrain'
constraint'
constrict'
constrict'ed
constric'tion
construct'
construct'ed
construc'tion
construct'ive
construct'ively
con'strue
con'strued
con'sul
con'sular
consult'
consult'ant
consulta'tion
consult'ed
consult'ing

consume'
consumed'
consu'mer
consum'mate
consumma'-
  tion
consump'tion
consump'tive
con'tact
conta'gion
conta'gious
contain'
contained'
contain'er
contam'inate
contam'inated
contam'inat-
  ing
contamina'-
  tion
con'template
con'templated
con'templating
contempla'tion
contempora'-
  neous
contem'porary
contempt'
contempt'ible
contemp'tuous
contemp'tu-
  ously
contend'
contend'ed
contend'er
con'tent,
  content'
content'ed
content'edly
conten'tion
content'ment
con'tents,
  contents'
(con'test, *n.*
(contest', *v.*
contest'ant
contest'ed
contest'ing

con'text
contig'uous
con'tinent
continen'tal
contin'gency
contin'gent
contin'gently
contin'ual
contin'uance
continua'tion
contin'ue
contin'ued
contin'uing
continu'ity
contin'uous
contin'uously
contin'uum
con'tour
con'tra
con'traband
contracep'tion
contracep'tive
(con'tract, n.
(contract', v.
contract'ed
contrac'tion
contract'or
contradict'
contradict'ed
contradic'tion
contradict'ory
contrap'tion
con'trary
(con'trast, n.
(contrast', v.
contrast'ed
contrast'ing
contravene'
contraven'tion
contrib'ute
contrib'uted
contrib'uting
contribu'tion
contrib'utor
contrib'utory
contri'vance
contrive'

control'
control'lable
controlled'
control'ler
control'ling
controver'sial
con'troversy
con'trovert
conun'drum
conurba'tion
convales'cence
convales'cent
convec'tor
convene'
convened'
conve'nience
conve'nient
conve'niently
con'vent
conven'tion
conven'tional
con'versant
conversa'tion
conversa'tional
(con'verse,
(n., adj.
(converse', v.
conversed'
con'versely
conver'sion
(con'vert, n.
(convert', v.
convert'ed
convert'ible
con'vex
convey'
convey'ance
convey'or
(con'vict, n.
(convict', v.
convict'ed
convict'ing
convic'tion
convince'
convinced'
convin'cing
conviv'ial

con'voy, *n.*	
convoy', *v.*	
convulse'	
convul'sion	
convul'sive	
cook	
cooked	
cook'er	
cook'ery	
cook'ing	
cool	
cool'ant	
cooled	
cool'er	
cool'est	
coo'lie	
cool'ly	
co-op'erate	
co-op'erated	
co-op'erating	
co-opera'tion	
co-op'erative	
co-op'erator	
co-opt'	
co-or'dinate, *v.*	
co-or'dinate, *n.a.*	
co-ordina'tion	
co-ord'inator	
copart'nership	
cope	
cop'ied	
co'-pi'lot	
co'ping	
co'pious	
cop'per	
cop'y	
cop'yholder	
cop'ying	
cop'yright	
cop'y-wri'ter	
cor'al	
cord	
cor'dial	
cordial'ity	
cor'don	
cor'duroy	
core	
cork	

cork'screw	
corn	
cor'ner	
cor'nice	
corol'lary	
corona'tion	
cor'oner	
cor'porate	
corpora'tion	
corps	
corpse	
cor'pulence	
cor'pulency	
cor'pulent	
cor'puscle	
correct'	
correct'ed	
correct'ing	
correc'tion	
correct'ive	
correct'ly	
correct'ness	
cor'relate	
cor'related	
correla'tion	
correspond'	
correspond'ed	
correspond'-ence	
correspond'ent	
correspond'ing	
cor'ridor	
corrob'orate	
corrob'orated	
corrob'orating	
corrobora'tion	
corrob'orative	
corrob'oratory	
corrode'	
corro'ded	
corro'sion	
corro'sive	
corrupt'	
corrup'tion	
cort'isone	
co'sily	

cosmet'ic	
cos'monaut	
cosmop'olis	
cosmopol'itan	
cost	
cost'liness	
cost'ly	
cos'tume	
co'sy	
co'terie	
cot'tage	
cot'ton	
couch	
cough	
coughed	
cough'ing	
could	
coun'cil	
coun'cillor, coun'cilor	
coun'sel	
coun'selled, coun'seled	
coun'sellor, coun'selor	
count	
count'ed	
coun'tenance	
count'er	
counteract'	
counteract'ed	
counter-bal'ance	
counter-bal'anced	
counterbal'-ancing	
coun'terblast	
count'erclaim	
count'erfeit	
count'erfeited	
count'erfeiter	
count'erfoil	
countermand'	
counter-mand'ed	
count'erpart	

count'ess	
count'ing	
count'ing-house	
count'less	
count'ry	
count'ryman	
coun'tryside	
count'y	
coupé'	
coup'le	
cou'pon	
cour'age	
coura'geous	
course	
coursed	
court	
court'eous	
court'esy	
court-mar'tial	
cous'in	
couture'	
couturier'	
cov'enant	
cov'er	
cov'er-charge	
cov'ered	
cov'ering	
cov'et	
cov'etous	
cow	
cow'ard	
cow'ardice	
coy	
co'zily	
co'zy	
crab	
crack	
cracked	
cra'dle	
craft	
craft'ily	
craft'iness	
crafts'man	
craft'y	
cram	
cramp	

cramped		cres'cent	
cran'berry		crest	
crane		cretonne'	
crank		crev'ice	
crash		crew	
crashed		crib	
crash'-landing		crick'et	
crate		crick'eter	
cra'ter		cried	
crave		crime	
craved		crim'inal	
cra'ving		crim'son	
crawl		crip'ple	
crawled		cri'sis	
cray'on		crisp	
craze		crite'rion	
crazed		crit'ic	
cra'zy		crit'ical	
creak		crit'icism	
creaked		crit'icize	
cream		crit'icized	
crease		cro'chet	
creased		cro'cheted	
create'		crock'ery	
crea'ted		crook	
crea'tion		crook'ed	
crea'tive		crop	
creativ'ity		crop'per	
crea'tor		croquette'	
crea'ture		cross	
cre'dence		crossed	
creden'tial		cross-examina'tion	
credibil'ity		cross-exam'ine	
cred'ible		cross-exam'ining	
cred'it		cross-ref'erence	
cred'itable		cross'roads	
cred'ited		cross'-sec'tion	
cred'iting		cross'word	
cred'itor		crowd	
credu'lity		crowd'ed	
cred'ulous		crowd'ing	
creed		crown	
creek		crowned	
creep		cru'cial	
creep'ing			
cre'ole			
crêpe			
crept			

cru'cifix	cu'mulative
crucifix'ion	cu'mulet
cru'cify	cun'ning
crude	cun'ningly
cru'dity	cup
cru'el	cup'board
cru'elly	cu'pro-nick'el
cru'elty	cur'able
cru'et	curb
cruise	cure
cruis'er	cured
crumb	cur'ing
crum'ble	cu'rio
crum'ple	curios'ity
crusade'	cu'rious
crush	cu'riously
crushed	curl
crust	curled
crust'ed	curl'y
crutch	cur'rant
crux	cur'rency
cry	cur'rent
cry'ing	cur'rently
crypt'ic	curric'ula
crys'tal	curric'ulum
crys'tallize	curse
Cu'ban	cursed
cube	curs'ed
cu'bic	cur'sive
cu'cumber	curs'or
cue	cur'sorily
cuff	cur'sory
cul'minate	curt
cul'minated	curtail'
	curtailed
culmina'tion	curtail'ment
culottes'	cur'tain
cul'pable	curt'ly
cul'prit	curv'ature
cul'tivate	curve
cul'tivated	curved
cultiva'tion	curv'ing
cul'tural	cush'ion
cul'ture	cus'tard
cul'tured	custo'dian
cul'vert	cus'tody
cum'bersome	cus'tom
cum'brous	

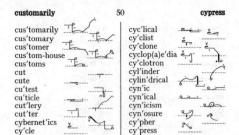

cus'tomarily	cyc'lical
cus'tomary	cy'clist
cus'tomer	cy'clone
cus'tom-house	cyclop(a)e'dia
cus'toms	cy'clotron
cut	cyl'inder
cute	cylin'drical
cu'test	cyn'ic
cu'ticle	cyn'ical
cut'lery	cyn'icism
cut'ter	cyn'osure
cybernet'ics	cy'pher
cy'cle	cy'press

D

dab'ble
dad
dad'dy
dai'ly
dain'ty
dai'ry
da'is
dai'sy
dam
dam'age
dam'aged
dam'aging
dam'ask
dame
damn
damp
damp'en
damp'er
damp'ness
dance
danced
dan'cer
dan'cing
dan'dy
dan'ger
dan'gerous
dan'gerously
Da'nish
dare
dared
dar'ing
dar'ingly
dark
dark'en
dark'er
dar'ling
darn
darned
dart
dart'ed

dash
dash'board
dashed
das'tardly
da'ta
date
da'ted
date'-line
daugh'ter
daunt
daunt'ed
daunt'less
dav'it
dawn
day
day'break
day'light
day'time
daze
daz'zle
daz'zled
dead
dead'beat
dead'en
dead'ened
dead'lock
deaf
deaf'-aid
deaf'en
deaf'ened
deal
deal'er
dealt
dean
dear
dear'er
dear'est
dearth
death
débâc'le

debag'		dec'imal	
debar'		dec'imate	
debarred'		decima'tion	
debar'ring		deci'pher	
debase'		deci'phered	
debased'		deci'sion	
deba'table		deci'sive	
debate'		deci'sively	
deba'ted		deck	
deba'ting		decked	
deben'ture		declara'tion	
debil'ity		declare'	
deb'it		declared'	
deb'ited		declar'ing	
deb'iting		declen'sion	
debonair'		decline'	
débris'		decli'ning	
debt		decliv'ity	
debt'or		declutch'	
debunk'		decode'	
début'		decompose'	
déb'utant		decomposed'	
		decomposi'tion	
déb'utante		decompress'	
		decontam'inate	
dec'ade		decontrol'	
dec'adence		dec'orate	
decay'		dec'orated	
decayed'		decora'tion	
decay'ing		dec'orative	
decease'		dec'orator	
deceased'		deco'rous	
deceit'		deco'rum	
deceit'ful		de'coy	
deceit'fulness		decoyed'	
deceive'		decoy'ing	
decel'erate		decrease'	
Decem'ber		decreased'	
de'cency		decree'	
de'cent		decreed'	
de'cently		decrep'it	
decentraliza'tion		decried'	
decen'tralize		decry'	
decep'tion		ded'icate	
decep'tive		ded'icated	
de'cibel		dedica'tion	
decide'		deduce'	
deci'ded		deduced'	
deci'dedly			

deduct′		defi′ciency	
deduct′ed		defi′cient	
deduct′ing		defi′ciently	
deduc′tion		def′icit	
deduct′ive		defied′	
deed		define′	
deem		defined′	
deemed		def′inite	
deep		def′initely	
deep′en		defini′tion	
deep′er		deflate′	
deep′est		defla′tion	
deep′ly		deflect′	
deer		deflect′ed	
deface′		deform′	
defaced′		deformed′	
deface′ment		deform′ity	
defal′cate		defraud′	
defalca′tion		defraud′ed	
defama′tion		defraud′ing	
defam′atory		defray′	
defame′		defrayed′	
default′		defray′ing	
default′ed		de′frost	
default′er		deft	
default′ing		deft′ly	
defeat′		defunct′	
defeat′ed		defy′	
defeat′ing		degen′erate,	
defeat′ist		*n. & a.*	
defect′		de′generate, *v.*	
defect′ive		degen′erated	
defence′		degrada′tion	
defend′		degrade′	
defend′ant		degra′ded	
defend′ed		degree′	
defen′sible		dehyd′rate	
defen′sive		deign	
defer′		deigned	
def′erence		de′ity	
deferen′tial		deject′	
defer′ment		deject′ed	
deferred′		dejec′tion	
defer′ring		delay′	
defi′ance		delayed′	
defi′ant		delay′ing	
		del′egate, *n.*	
		dele′gate, *v.*	

del'egated	
del'egating	
delega'tion	
delete'	
delete'rious	
dele'tion	
delib'erate, *adj.*	
delib'erate, *v.*	
delibera'tion	
del'icacy	
del'icate	
delicatess'en	
deli'cious	
delight'	
delight'ed	
delight'ful	
delin'eate	
delinea'tion	
delin'quency	
delin'quent	
delir'ious	
delir'ium	
deliv'er	
deliv'erance	
deliv'ered	
deliv'ering	
deliv'ery	
del'ta-wing	
delude'	
delu'ded	
delu'ding	
del'uge	
delu'sion	
delve	
demand'	
demand'ed	
demand'ing	
demarca'tion	
demean'our, demean'or	
demerar'a	
demo'bilize	
democ'racy	
dem'ocrat	
democrat'ic	
demol'ish	
demol'ished	

demoli'tion	
demonetiza'tion	
demon'strate	
demon'strated	
demon'strating	
demonstra'tion	
demon'strative	
dem'onstrator	
demor'alize	
demor'alized	
demor'alizing	
demo'tion	
demur'	
demure'	
demur'rage	
demurred'	
demy'	
deni'al	
denied'	
de'nim	
denom'inating	
denomina'tion	
denomina'tional	
denote'	
deno'ted	
deno'ting	
denounce'	
denounced'	
dense	
dense'ly	
den'sity	
dent	
den'tal	
den'tifrice	
den'tist	
den'tistry	
denuncia'tion	
deny'	
deo'dorize	
depart'	
depart'ed	
depart'ing	
depart'ment	
department'al	
depar'ture	

depend'	derange'ment	
depend'able	der'elict	
depend'ed	derelic'tion	
depend'ence	deride'	
depend'ent	deri'ded	
deplete'	deri'sion	
deple'ted	deri'sive	
deple'ting	deriva'tion	
deple'tion	deriv'ative	
deplor'able	derive'	
deplore'	deri'ving	
deplored'	descend'	
deplor'ing	descend'ant	
deport'	descend'ed	
deport'ed	descent'	
deport'ment	describe'	
depose'	descri'bing	
deposed'	descried'	
depos'it	descrip'tion	
depos'itary	descrip'tions	
depos'ited	descrip'tive	
depos'iting	descry'	
deposi'tion	des'ecrate	
depos'itor	desecra'tion	
depos'itory	{des'ert, *n.*,	
dep'ot	*adj.*	
depraved'	desert', *v.*	
deprav'ity	desert'ed	
dep'recate	desert'er	
dep'recated	desert'ing	
depre'ciate	deser'tion	
depre'ciated	deserve'	
depre'ciating	deserv'edly	
deprecia'tion	deserv'ing	
depress'	desidera'tum	
depressed'	design'	
depres'sion	des'ignate	
depriva'tion	des'ignated	
deprive'	designa'tion	
deprived'	designed'	
depth	design'er	
deputa'tion	desirabil'ity	
depute'	desir'able	
depu'ted	desire'	
depu'ting	desired'	
dep'utize	desir'ing	
dep'uty	desir'ous	
derange'	desist'	

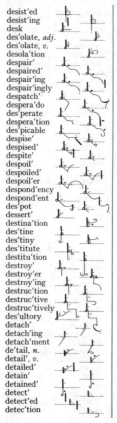
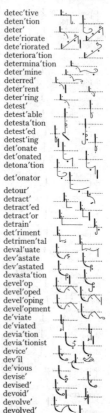

desist'ed
desist'ing
desk
des'olate, *adj.*
des'olate, *v.*
desola'tion
despair'
despaired'
despair'ing
despair'ingly
despatch'
despera'do
des'perate
despera'tion
des'picable
despise'
despised'
despite'
despoil'
despoiled'
despoil'er
despond'ency
despond'ent
des'pot
dessert'
destina'tion
des'tine
des'tiny
des'titute
destitu'tion
destroy'
destroy'er
destroy'ing
destruc'tion
destruc'tive
destruc'tively
des'ultory
detach'
detach'ing
detach'ment
de'tail, *n.*
detail', *v.*
detailed'
detain'
detained'
detect'
detect'ed
detec'tion

detec'tive
deten'tion
deter'
dete'riorate
dete'riorated
deteriora'tion
determina'tion
deter'mine
deterred'
deter'rent
deter'ring
detest'
detest'able
detesta'tion
detest'ed
detest'ing
det'onate
det'onated
detona'tion
det'onator
detour'
detract'
detract'ed
detract'or
detrain'
det'riment
detrimen'tal
deval'uate
dev'astate
dev'astated
devasta'tion
devel'op
devel'oped
devel'oping
devel'opment
de'viate
de'viated
devia'tion
devia'tionist
device'
dev'il
de'vious
devise'
devised'
devoid'
devolve'
devolved'

devolv'ing	
devote'	
devo'ted	
devo'tedly	
devotee'	
devo'ting	
devo'tion	
devour'	
devoured'	
devour'ing	
devout'	
dew	
dexter'ity	
dex'terous	
diabe'tes	
diabol'ic	
diagnose'	
diagno'sis	
diag'onal	
di'agram	
di'al	
di'alect	
di'alling, di'aling	
di'alogue	
diam'eter	
diamet'ric	
diamet'rical	
di'amond	
di'aphragm	
di'arist	
di'ary	
{dic'tate, *n.*	
{dictate', *v.*	
dicta'ted	
dicta'ting	
dicta'tion	
dicta'tor	
dictato'rial	
dicta'torship	
dic'tion	
dic'tionary	
dic'tum	
did	
die	
died	
die'hard	
di'et	

di'etary	
di'eted	
dietet'ics	
di'eting	
dif'fer	
dif'fered	
dif'ference	
dif'ferent	
differen'tiate	
dif'ferently	
dif'ficult	
dif'ficulty	
dif'fidence	
dif'fident	
diffuse'	
diffused'	
diffu'sion	
dig	
di'gest, *n.*	
digest', *v.*	
digest'ed	
digest'ible	
digest'ing	
diges'tion	
diges'tive	
dig'it	
dig'nify	
dig'nity	
digress'	
digres'sion	
dike	
dilap'idate	
dilap'idated	
dilapida'tion	
dilap'idator	
dilata'tion	
dilate'	
dil'atory	
dilem'ma	
dil'igence	
dil'igent	
dil'igently	
dilute'	
dilu'ted	
dilu'tion	
dim	

dimen'sion	disagree'ing
dimin'ish	disagree'ment
dimin'ished	disallow'
diminu'tion	disappear'
dimin'utive	disappear'ance
dimmed	disappeared'
din	disappear'ing
dine	disappoint'
di'ner	disappoint'ed
din'gey,	disappoint'ing
din'ghy	disappoint'-
din'gy	ment
di'ning	disapproba'-
di'ning-room	tion
din'ner	disapprov'al
dint	disapprove'
di'ocese	disapprov'ing
di'ode	disarm'
dip	disarm'ament
di'phone	disarmed'
diphthe'ria	disarrange'
diph'thong	disarranged'
diplo'ma	disas'ter
diplo'macy	disas'trous
dip'lomat	disas'trously
diplomat'ic	disband'
dire	disband'ed
direct'	disbelief'
direct'ed	disbelieve'
direc'tion	disbelieved'
direct'or	disburse'
direct'orate	disbursed'
direct'ory	disburse'ment
dirn'dl	disc
dirt	discard'
dirt'y	discard'ed
disabil'ity	discard'ing
disa'ble	discern'
disa'blement	discerned'
disa'bling	discern'ible
disadvan'tage	discern'ing
disadvanta'-	discern'ment
geous	discharge'
disadvanta'-	discharged'
geously	discharg'ing
disagree'	disci'ple
disagree'able	disciplina'rian
disagreed'	dis'ciplinary

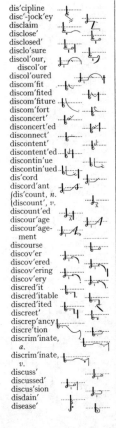

dis'cipline
disc'-jock'ey
disclaim
disclose
disclosed'
disclo'sure
discol'our,
  discol'or
discol'oured
discom'fit
discom'fited
discom'fiture
discom'fort
disconcert'
disconcert'ed
disconnect'
discontent'
discontent'ed
discontin'ue
discontin'ued
dis'cord
discord'ant
(dis'count, *n.*
(discount', *v.*
discount'ed
discour'age
discour'age-
  ment
discourse
discov'er
discov'ered
discov'ering
discov'ery
discred'it
discred'itable
discred'ited
discreet'
discrep'ancy
discre'tion
discrim'inate,
  a.
discrim'inate,
  v.
discuss'
discussed'
discus'sion
disdain'
disease'

diseased'
disembark'
disembarka'-
  tion
disestab'lish
disestab'-
  lished
disestab'lish-
  ment
disfa'vour,
  disfa'vor
disfig'ure
disfig'urement
disfig'uring
disfran'chise
disgorge'
disgrace'
disgraced'
disgrace'ful
disgrace'fully
disgrun'tled
disguise'
disguised'
disgust'
disgust'ed
disgust'ing
dish
disheart'en
disheart'ened
disheart'ening
dishev'el
dishev'elled,
  dishev'eled
dishon'est
dishon'estly
dishon'esty
dishon'our,
  dishon'or
dishon'ourable
dishon'oured
disillu'sion
disincen'tive
disinclina'tion
disinclined'
disinfect'
disinfect'ant
disinfect'ed

disinher'it	dispersed'
disinher'itance	dispers'ing
disinher'ited	displace'
disin'tegrate	displaced'
disin'tegrated	displace'ment
disintegra'tion	display'
disin'terested	displayed'
disjoint'ed	display'ing
dislike'	displease'
disliked'	displeased'
dis'locate	displeas'ure
dis'located	dispo'sal
dis'locating	dispose'
disloca'tion	disposed'
disloy'al	disposi'tion
dis'mal	dispossess'
disman'tle	dispossessed'
disman'tled	dispropor'-
dismay'	tionate
dismiss'	disprove'
dismiss'al	disput'able
dismissed'	dis'putant
dismiss'ing	dispute'
dismount'	dispu'ted
dismount'ed	dispu'ting
disobe'dience	disqualifica'-
disobe'dient	tion
disobey'	disqual'ify
disor'der	disqual'ifying
disor'derly	disregard'
disorganiza'-	disregard'ed
tion	disrep'utable
disor'ganize	disrepute'
disor'ganized	disrespect'
disown'	disrespect'ful
disowned'	disrup'tion
dispar'age	dis_satisfac'tion_
dispar'age-	dissat'isfied
ment	dissect'
dispatch'	dissec'tion
dispatch'ing	dissent'
dispen'sary	dissent'ed
dispensa'tion	dissim'ilar
dispense'	dis'sipate
dispensed'	dis'sipated
dispen'sing	dissipa'tion
dispers'al	dissolu'tion
disperse'	dissolve'

dissuade'	ditch
dissua'ded	dit'to
dis'tance	divan'
dis'tant	dive
dis'tantly	di'ver
distaste'	diverge'
distaste'ful	diver'gent
distem'per	di'vers
distil', distill'	diverse'
distilled'	diver'sified
distil'lery	diver'sion
distinct'	diver'sity
distinc'tion	divert'
distinct'ive	divert'ed
distinct'ively	divide'
distinct'ly	divi'ded
distin'guish	div'idend
distin'guish-	divi'ding
able	divine'
distin'guished	divine'ly
distin'guishing	divin'ity
distort'	divis'ible
distort'ed	divi'sion
distor'tion	divi'sional
distract'	divorce'
distract'ed	divorced'
distrac'tion	divorcee'
distrain'	divulge'
distress'	diz'zy
distressed'	*do*
distress'ful	do'cile
distrib'ute	dock
distrib'uted	docker
distrib'uter	dock'et
distrib'uting	dock'yard
distribu'tion	doc'tor
distrib'utor	doc'trine
dis'trict	doc'ument
distrust'	documen'tary
distrust'ed	dod'derer
distrust'ful	dodge
disturb'	does, *v.*
disturb'ance	dog
disturbed'	dog'ma
disturb'ing	dogmat'ic
disuse', *n.*	*do'ing*
disuse', *v.*	dole
disused'	dole'ful

doll	down'cast
dol'lar	down'fall
domain'	down'hearted
dome	down'hill
domes'tic	down'pour
domes'ticate	down'right
domes'ticated	down'stairs
dom'icile	down'wards
dom'inant	doze
dom'inate	dozed
dom'inated	doz'en
domina'tion	drab
domineer'ing	drachm
Domin'ican	draft
domin'ion	draft'ed
donate'	drag
dona'ted	drain
dona'ting	drain'age
dona'tion	drake
done	dram
do'nor	dra'ma
doo'dle	dramat'ic
doom	dram'atist
door	drank
door'step	drape
door'way	dra'per
dope	dras'tic
dor'mant	dras'tically
dor'mitory	draught
dose	draughts'man
dot	draught'y
dot'ted	draw
dot'ting	drawee'
doub'le	draw'er
doubt	draw'ing
doubt'ed	drawl
doubt'ful	drawn
doubt'fully	dray
doubt'ing	dread
doubt'ingly	dread'ed
doubt'less	dread'ful
doubts	dread'ing
douche	dread'nought
dough	dream
dough'nut	dreamed
dove'tail	dreamt'
dove'tailed	drear'y
down	dredge

dredg'er	dubi'ety
dregs	du'bious
drench	du'cal
Dres'den	duch'ess
dress	duch'y
dress'er	duck
dress'maker	duc'tile
dried	due
dri'er	du'el
drift	duet'
drift'ed	dug
drift'ing	duke
drill	dull
drilled	du'ly
drink	dumb
drink'er	dumbfound'
drip	dumbfound'ed
drive	dump
driv'el	dun
driv'en	dunce
dri'ver	dune
dri'ving	dun'ning
driz'zle	duoden'al
drom'edary	dupe
drone	du'plex
droop	du'plicate,
drop	*n. & a.*
dross	du'plicate, *v.*
drought	du'plicated
drouth	duplica'tion
drove	du'plicator
drown	duplic'ity
drow'siness	durabil'ity
drow'sy	du'rable
drudge	dural'umin
drudg'ery	dura'tion
drug	dur'ing
drug'gist	dusk
drum	dusk'y
drum'mer	dust
drunk	dust'ed
drunk'ard	dust'er
drunk'en	Dutch
drunk'enness	du'tiable
dry	du'tiful
dry'clean	du'ty
dry'-rot	dwarf
du'al	

dwarfed
dwell
dwell'er
dwell'ing
dwell'ing-
  house
dwelt
dwin'dle
dwin'dled
dwin'dling
dye
dye'ing

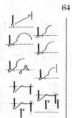

dy'er
dy'ing
dynam'ic
dy'namite
dy'namo
dy'namotor
dy'nasty
dysenter'ic
dys'entery
dyspep'sia
dyspep'tic
dyspros'ium

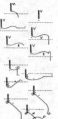

E

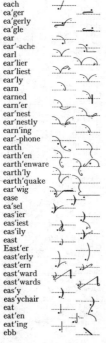

each
ea'ger
ea'gerly
ea'gle
ear
ear'-ache
earl
ear'lier
ear'liest
ear'ly
earn
earned
earn'er
ear'nest
ear'nestly
earn'ing
ear'-phone
earth
earth'en
earth'enware
earth'ly
earth'quake
ear'wig
ease
ea'sel
eas'ier
eas'iest
eas'ily
east
East'er
east'erly
east'ern
east'ward
east'wards
eas'y
eas'ychair
eat
eat'en
eat'ing
ebb

ebbed
ebb'tide
eb'ony
eccen'tric
eccentric'ity
ecclesias'tic
ech'o
ech'oed
ech'oing
éc'lair'
eclipse'
econom'ic
econom'ical
econom'ics
econ'omist
econ'omize
econ'omy
cc'stasy
ecstat'ic
ec'toplasm
edge
edg'y
ed'ible
e'dict
edifica'tion
ed'ifice
ed'ified
ed'ify
ed'it
ed'ited
ed'iting
edi'tion
ed'itor
edito'rial
ed'itorship
ed'ucate
ed'ucated
educa'tion
educa'tional
educa'tionalist

educa'tionist	el'derly
ed'ucator	el'dest
eel	elect'
ee'rie, ee'ry	elect'ed
efface'	elec'tion
efface'ment	elect'or
effect'	elect'oral
effect'ed	elect'orate
effect'ing	elec'tric
effect'ive	elec'trical
effect'ively	elec'trically
effects'	electri'cian
effec'tual	electric'ity
effem'inate	electrifica'tion
effervesce'	elec'trified
efferves'cent	elec'trify
effica'cious	elec'trocute
ef'ficacy	elec'trocuted
effi'ciency	electrol'ysis
effi'cient	elec'tron
ef'fort	electron'ic
ef'fortless	electron'ics
egg	el'egance
Egyp'tian	el'egant
eh	el'egantly
ei'derdown	el'ement
eight	elemen'tary
eighteen	el'ephant
eighteenth	el'evate
eighth	el'evated
eight'ieth	eleva'tion
eight'y	el'evator
ei'ther	elev'en
ejac'ulate	elev'enth
ejac'ulated	elic'it
ejacula'tion	elic'ited
eject'	eligibil'ity
eject'ed	el'igible
ejec'tion	elim'inate
elab'orate, *adj.*	elim'inated
elab'orate, *v.*	elim'inating
elab'orately	elimina'tion
elabora'tion	Elizabe'than
elapse'	elm
elas'tic	elocu'tion
elastic'ity	elocu'tionist
el'bow	e'longate
el'der	e'longated

elonga'tion	embroca'tion
elope'	embroid'er
elope'ment	embroid'ery
el'oquence	em'bryo
el'oquent	emend'
el'oquently	emenda'tion
else	em'erald
else'where	emerge'
elu'cidate	emer'gency
elu'cidated	em'ery
elucida'tion	emet'ic
elude'	em'igrant
elu'sive	em'igrate
elu'sively	em'igrated
ema'ciate	emigra'tion
ema'ciated	em'inence
em'anate	em'inent
em'anating	em'inently
eman'cipate	em'issary
emancipa'tion	emis'sion
embalm'	emit'
embalmed'	emol'ument
	emo'tion
embank'ment	emo'tional
embar'go	em'pathy
embark'	em'peror
embarka'tion	em'phasis
embar'rass	em'phasize
embar'rass-ment	em'phasized
em'bassy	emphat'ic
embed'	emphat'ically
embed'ded	em'pire
embel'lish	empir'ical
embel'lish-ment	employ'
embez'zle	employ'able
embez'zled	employee'
embez'zle-ment	employees'
embez'zler	employ'er
embit'ter	employ'ing
em'blem	employ'ment
embod'ied	empo'rium
embod'iment	empow'er
embod'y	empow'ered
emboss'	em'press
embrace'	emp'tied
	emp'ty
	emp'tying
	em'ulate

emula'tion		endeav'our,	
emul'sion		endeav'or	
ena'ble		end'ed	
ena'bled		end'less	
ena'bling		end'lessly	
enact'		endorse'	
enact'ed		endorse'ment	
enact'ment		endow'	
enam'el		endowed'	
enam'elled,		endow'ment	
enam'eled		endur'able	
enam'our,		endur'ance	
enam'or		endure'	
enam'oured		endured'	
encamp'		en'emy	
encamped'		energet'ic	
encamp'ment		en'ergy	
encase'		en'ervate	
encased'		en'ervated	
encash'ment		enfold'	
enchant'		enfold'ed	
enchant'ed		enfold'ing	
enchant'ment		enforce'	
encir'cle		enforced'	
enclose'		enforce'ment	
enclosed'		enforc'ing	
enclo'sure		enfran'chise	
encoun'ter		enfran'chise-	
encoun'tered		ment	
encount'ering		engage'	
encour'age		engage'ment	
encour'age-		engen'der	
ment		engen'dered	
encour'aging		en'gine	
encroach'		engineer'	
encroached'		engineered'	
encroach'ing		engineer'ing	
encroach'ment		Eng'lish	
encrust'		Eng'lishman	
encrust'ed		Eng'lishwoman	
encum'ber		engrave'	
encum'bered		engraved'	
encum'brance		engra'ver	
encyclope'dia		engra'ving	
end		engross'	
endan'ger		engrossed'	
endan'gering		enhance'	
endear		enhanced'	

enhance'ment
enhan'cing
enig'ma
enigmat'ic
enjoin'
enjoy'
enjoy'able
enjoy'ment
enlarge'
enlarged'
enlarge'ment
enlar'ger
enlar'ging
enlight'en
enlight'ened
enlight'enment
enlist'
enlist'ed
enlist'ing
enlist'ment
enli'ven
enli'vened
en'mity
enor'mity
enor'mous
enough'
enquire'
enquired'
enquir'y
enrage'
enrich'
enrol', enroll'
enrolled'
enrol'ment
enshrine'
en'sign
ensue'
ensued'
ensu'ing
ensure'
entail'
entailed'
entan'gle
entan'gled
entan'glement
en'ter
en'tered
en'terprise

entertain'
entertained'
entertain'er
entertain'ment
enthuse'
enthu'siasm
enthu'siast
enthusias'tic
enthusias'tic-ally
entice'
enticed'
entice'ment
entire'
entire'ly
entire'ty
enti'tle
enti'tled
enti'tling
{en'trance, *n.*
{entrance', *v.*
entranced'
entranc'ing
en'trant
entreat'
entreat'ed
entreat'y
entrust'
entrust'ed
entrust'ing
en'try
enu'merate
enu'merated
enumera'tion
enun'ciate
enun'ciated
enuncia'tion
envel'op
en'velope
en'viable
en'vied
en'vious
envi'ronment
envis'age
en'voy
en'vy
en'zyme
ep'ic

epicen'tre
epidem'ic
ep'ilogue
epis'copal
ep'isode
epis'tle
ep'itaph
ep'ithet
epit'ome
ep'och
e'quable
e'qual
equalitar'ian
equal'ity
equaliza'tion
e'qualize
e'qualized
e'qualled, e'qualed
e'qualling, e'qualing
e'qually
equa'tor
eq'uerry
eques'trian
equilib'rium
e'quine
equip'
equip'ment
equipped'
eq'uitable
eq'uity
equiv'alent
equiv'ocal
e'ra
erad'icate
erase'
era'ser
era'sure
ere
erect'
erec'tion
ergonom'ics
er'mine
erode'
ero'sion
err
er'rand
erra'ta
errat'ic
erra'tum
erred
err'ing
erro'neous
erro'neously
er'ror
erst'while
er'udite
erudi'tion
erup'tion
es'calator
escape'
eschew'
eschewed'
es'cort, *n.*
escort', *v.*
escort'ed
espe'cial
espe'cially
espy'
esquire'
es'say
essayed'
es'sayist
es'sence
essen'tial
estab'lish
estab'lished
estab'lishing
estab'lishment
estate'
esteem'
esteemed'
es'timable
es'timate, *n.*
es'timate, *v.*
es'timated
estima'tion
estrange'
estrange'ment
es'tuary
et cet'era, etc.
etch
etch'er
etch'ing
eter'nal

eter′nity	
e′ther	
ethe′real	
eth′ical	
eth′ics	
eth′yl	
et′iquette	
etymolog′ical	
etymol′ogy	
Euclid	
eugen′ic	
eu′logy	
euphor′ia	
Europe′an	
evac′uate	
evacua′tion	
evade′	
eval′uate	
evalua′tion	
evan′gelist	
evap′orate	
evap′orated	
evapora′tion	
eva′sion	
eva′sive	
eve	
e′ven	
eve′ning	
e′venly	
e′vensong	
event′	
event′ful	
even′tual	
eventual′ity	
even′tually	
ev′er	
everlast′ing	
everlast′ingly	
ev′ery	
ev′erybody	
ev′erything	
everywhere	
evict′	
evic′tion	
ev′idence	
ev′ident	
ev′idently	
e′vil	

evince′	
evoke′	
evoked′	
evolu′tion	
evolve′	
ewe	
ew′er	
exact′	
exact′ly	
exag′gerate	
exaggera′tion	
exalt′	
exalt′ed	
exalta′tion	
examina′tion	
exam′ine	
exam′iner	
exam′ining	
exam′ple	
exas′perate	
exas′perated	
exaspera′tion	
ex′cavate	
ex′cavated	
excava′tion	
exceed′	
exceed′ingly	
excel′	
excelled′	
ex′cellence	
ex′cellent	
ex′cellently	
excel′sior	
except′	
except′ed	
except′ing	
excep′tion	
excep′tional	
ex′cerpt	
excess′	
excess′ive	
excess′ively	
exchange′	
exchanged′	
exchang′ing	
excise′	
excite′	
excite′ment	

exclaim'	exhort'ed
exclaimed'	ex'igency
exclama'tion	ex'ile
exclude'	ex'iled
exclu'sion	exist'
exclu'sive	exist'ed
exclu'sively	exist'ence
excru'ciate	exist'ent
excur'sion	existen'tial
excu'sable	exist'ing
{excuse', n.	ex'it
{excuse', v.	exor'bitant
excused'	expand'
ex'ecute	expand'ed
ex'ecuted	expanse'
execu'tion	expan'sion
exec'utive	expan'sionist
exec'utor	expan'sive
exec'utrix	
exem'plary	expect'
exem'plify	expect'ed
exempt'	expect'ant
exemp'tion	expect'antly
ex'ercise	expecta'tion
ex'ercised	expect'ing
exert'	expe'diency
exert'ed	expe'dient
exer'tion	expe'diently
exhale'	ex'pedite
exhaled'	ex'pedited
exha'ling	expedi'tion
exhaust'	expel'
exhaust'ed	expelled'
exhaust'ing	expend'
exhaustion	expend'ed
exhaust'ive	expend'iture
exhaust'ively	expense'
exhib'it	expen'sive
exhib'ited	expen'sively
exhib'iting	expe'rience
exhibi'tion	expe'riencing
exhibi'tionist	exper'iment
exhib'itor	experimen'tal
exhil'arate	ex'pert
exhil'arated	expertise'
exhilara'tion	expira'tion
exhort'	expire'
exhorta'tion	expired'

expi'ry	
explain'	
explained'	
explana'tion	
explan'atory	
explic'it	
explode'	
explo'ded	
exploit'	
exploita'tion	
explora'tion	
explore'	
explored'	
explor'er	
explo'sion	
explo'sive	
expo'nent	
ex'port, *n.*	
export', *v.*	
export'ed	
export'er	
export'ing	
expose'	
exposi'tion	
expo'sure	
express'	
expres'sion	
express'ive	
express'ly	
expul'sion	
ex'quisite	
ex'tant	
extempora'-neous	
extend'	
extend'ed	
exten'sion	
exten'sive	
extent'	
exten'uate	
exten'uating	
extenua'tion	
exte'rior	
exter'minate	
extermina'tion	
exter'nal	
extinct'	

extinc'tion	
extin'guish	
extin'guished	
extin'guisher	
extol'	
extolled'	
extor'tion	
ex'tra	
ex'tract, *n.*	
extract', *v.*	
extract'ed	
extrac'tion	
ex'tradite	
ex'tradited	
ex'tradting	
extradi'tion	
extra'neous	
extraor'din-arily	
extraor'dinary	
extrav'agance	
extrav'agant	
extrav'agantly	
extreme'	
extrem'ity	
ex'tricate	
ex'tricated	
ex'trovert	
exu'berance	
exu'berant	
exude'	
exult'	
exulta'tion	
exult'ed	
eye	
eye'ball	
eye'brow	
eyed	
eye'ing, ey'ing	
eye'lash	
eye'lid	
eye'-op'ener	
eyes	
eye'sight	
eye'sore	
eye'wash	
eye'-witness	

F

fa'ble
fab'ric
fab'ricate
fabrica'tion
fab'ulous
façade'
face
fac'et
face'tious
face'tiously
fa'cial
fac'ile
facil'itate
facil'itated
facil'ity
facsim'ile
fact
fac'tion
fac'tious
fac'tor
fac'tory
fac'tual
fac'ulty
fad
fad'dist
fade
fade'-out
fag
Fah'renheit
fail
failed
fail'ing
fail'ure
faint
faint'ed
faintheart'ed
faint'ly
fair
fair'er
fair'est

fair'ly
fair'ness
fair'y
faith
faith'ful
faith'fully
faith'fulness
faith'lessness
fake
faked
fall
falla'cious
fal'lacy
fall'en
fall'ing
fall'-out
false
false'hood
false'ly
falset'to
falsifica'tion
fal'sified
fal'sify
fal'ter
fal'tered
fal'tering
fame
famed
famil'iar
familiar'ity
familiariza'-
    tion
famil'iarize
famil'iarizing
famil'iarly
fam'ily
fam'ine
fam'ish

74

fam'ished	fatal'ity
fam'ishing	fa'tally
fa'mous	fate
fan	fate'ful
fanat'ic	fa'ther
fanat'ical	fa'ther-*in*-law
fanat'icism	fa'therland
fan'cied	fa'therless
fan'ciful	fath'om
fan'cifully	fatigue'
fan'cy	fat'ten
fantas'tic	fatu'ity
fantas'tical	fat'uous
	fault
fantas'tically	fault'less
fan'tasy	fault'y
far	fau'na
farce	fa'vour, fa'vor
far'cical	fa'vourable
fare	fa'voured
fared	fa'vourite
farewell'	fa'vouritism
	fawn
farina'ceous	fear
farm	feared
farmed	fear'ful
farm'er	fear'ing
farm'house	fear'less
far'sighted	feasibil'ity
far'ther	fea'sible
far'thest	fea'sibly
farth'ing	feast
fas'cinate	feast'ing
fascina'tion	feat
fash'ion	feath'er
fash'ionable	feath'ery
fash'ioned	fea'ture
fast	fea'tured
fast'en	fea'tureless
fast'ened	Feb'ruary
fast'ener	fed
fast'er	fed'eral
fast'est	fed'eralism
fastid'ious	fed'eralist
fast'ing	federa'tion
fat	fee
fa'tal	fee'ble
fa'talism	feed
fa'talist	

feed'er	
feed'ing	
feel	
feel'ing	
feel'ingly	
feet	
feign	
feint	
felic'itate	
felic'itated	
felicita'tion	
felic'itous	
felic'ity	
fe'line	
fell	
felled	
fel'low	
fel'lowship	
fel'on	
felo'nious	
felo'niously	
fel'ony	
felt	
fe'male	
fem'inine	
fem'inism	
fence	
fenced	
fen'cer	
fend'er	
{fer'ment, *n.*	
{ferment', *v.*	
fermenta'tion	
ferment'ed	
fern	
fero'cious	
feroc'ity	
ferroconc'rete	
fer'ry	
fer'tile	
fertil'ity	
fertiliza'tion	
fer'tilize	
fer'tilizer	
fer'vent	
fer'vently	
fer'vid	

fer'vour, fer'-vor	
fes'ter	
fes'tered	
fes'tival	
fes'tive	
festiv'ity	
fetch	
fetch'ing	
fet'ter	
fet'tered	
feud	
feu'dal	
feuds	
fe'ver	
fe'verish	
fe'verishly	
few	
few'er	
fiancé, fiancée	
fias'co	
fi'at	
fib	
fi'bre	
fi'breglass	
fibrosit'is	
fi'brous	
fick'le	
fic'tion	
ficti'tious	
fid'dle	
fidel'ity	
fidg'et	
fidg'ety	
fidu'ciary	
field	
fiend	
fiend'ish	
fierce	
fierc'est	
fi'ery	
fi'es'ta	
fifteen'	
fifteenth'	
fifth	
fif'ty	
fig	

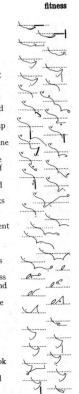

fight
fight'er
fight'ing
fig'ment
fig'urative
fig'uratively
fig'ure
fig'urehead
figurine'
fil'ament
filch
file
filed
fil'ial
fi'ling
fill
filled
fill'er
fil'let
fil'leted
fill'ing
fill'ip
film
fil'ter
fil'tered
filth
fil'trate
filtra'tion
fin
fi'nal
final'ity
fi'nally
finance'
financed'
finan'cial
finan'cially
finan'cier
find
find'er
find'ing
fine
fined
fine'drawn
fine'ly
fi'ner
fi'nery
finesse'
fi'nest

fin'ger
fin'gered
fin'ical
fi'nis
fin'ish
fin'ished
fin'ishing
fir
fire
fire'arms
fire'brand
fire'clay
fire'-damp
fired
fire'-engine
fire'man
fire'place
fire'proof
fire'side
fire'wood

fire'works
fir'ing
firm
fir'mament
firm'er
firm'ly
firm'ness
first
first'-class
first'-hand
first'ly
first'-rate
firth
fis'cal
fish
fished
fish'er
fish'ery
fish'-hook
fis'sure
fis'sured
fist
fit
fit'ful
fit'ly
fit'ness

fit′ted		flaunt′ed	
fit′ter		fla′vour,	
fit′test		fla′vor	
fit′ting		fla′voured	
fit′tingly		fla′vouring	
five		flaw	
fiv′er		flaw′less	
fix		flax	
fixa′tion		flay	
fixed		flea	
fix′edly		fled	
fix′ture		flee	
fiz′zle		fleece	
fiz′zled		fleet	
flab′by		flesh	
flac′cid		flew	
flag		flexibil′ity	
flag′on		flex′ible	
fla′grant		flick	
fla′grantly		flick′er	
flag′-ship		flick′ered	
flake		fli′er	
flaked		flight	
flamboy′ant		flight′y	
flame		flim′sily	
flan		flim′sy	
flange		flinch	
flank		fling	
flan′nel		flint	
flannelette		flip′pancy	
flap		flip′pant	
flap′per		flip′pantly	
flare		flirt	
flared		flirt′ing	
flash		flit	
flashed		flit′ted	
flask		flit′ting	
flat		float	
flat′ly		float′ed	
flat′ten		flock	
flat′tened		flocked	
flat′ter		flog	
flat′tered		flogged	
flat′terer		flood	
flat′tery		flood′ing	
flat′ulence		flood′light	
flat′ulent		floor	
flaunt		floor′ing	

flop	flut'tered	
flo'ral	flux	
flor'id	fly	
flor'in	fly'er	
flor'ist	fly'leaf	
floss	fly'over	
flota'tion	fly'-wheel	
flotil'la	foam	
flot'sam	fob	
flounce	fo'cus	
floun'der	fo'cus(s)ed	
floun'dered	fod'der	
flour	foe	
flour'ish	fog	
flour'ished	fogged	
flour'ishing	fog'gy	
flout	foil	
flout'ed	foiled	
flow	foist	
flowed	fold	
flow'er	fold'ed	
flow'ered	fold'er	
flow'ery	fold'ing	
flow'ing	fo'liage	
flown	fo'lio	
fluc'tuate	folk	
fluc'tuated	folk'lore	
fluc'tuating	fol'low	
fluctua'tion	fol'lowed	
flue	fol'lower	
flu'ency	fol'lowing	
flu'ent	fol'ly	
flu'ently	foment'	
fluff	fomenta'tion	
fluff'y	fond	
flu'id	fond'er	
fluke	fond'est	
flung	fon'dle	
flunk'ey	fon'dled	
fluores'cent	fond'ly	
flur'ried	food	
flur'ry	food'stuff	
flush	fool	
flushed	fooled	
flus'ter	fool'hardy	
flus'tered	fool'ish	
flute	fool'ishly	
flut'ter	fools'cap	

foot		fore'noon	
foot'ball		forerun'ner	
foot'board		foresee'	
foot'hold		foresee'able	
foot'ing		foreseen'	
foot'lights		foreshad'ow	
foot'mark		fore'sight	
foot'note		for'est	
foot'print		forestall'	
foot'sore		forestalled'	
foot'step		for'ester	
foot'stool		for'estry	
for		foretell'	
for'age		fore'thought	
for'ay		foretold'	
forbad', for-		*forev*'er	
bade'		forewarn'	
{for'bear, *n.*		forewarned'	
{forbear', *v.*		fore'word	
forbear'ance		for'feit	
forbid'		for'feited	
forbid'den		for'feiture	
force		forgave'	
forced		forge	
force'ful		for'ger	
for'ceps		for'gery	
for'cible		forget'	
ford		forget'ful	
ford'ed		forget'fulness	
fore		forgive'	
fore'arm		forgive'ness	
forebo'ding		forgiv'ing	
{fore'cast, *n.*		forgo'	
{forecast', *v.*		forgot'	
foreclose'		forgot'ten	
foreclo'sure		fork	
fore'court		forlorn'	
fore'father		form	
forego'		form'al	
forego'ing		formal'ity	
foregone'		forma'tion	
fore'ground		formed	
fore'hand		for'mer	
fore'head		for'merly	
for'eign		for'midable	
for'eigner		for'mula	
fore'man		for'mulate	
fore'most		forsake'	

forsa'ken		fox	
forsook'		fracas	
fort		frac'tion	
forth		frac'tious	
forth'coming		frac'ture	
forth'right		frac'tured	
forthwith'		frag'ile	
for'tieth		fragil'ity	
fortifica'tion		frag'ment	
for'tified		frag'mentary	
for'tify		fra'grance	
for'titude		fra'grant	
fort'night		frail	
fort'nightly		frail'ty	
for'tress		frame	
fortu'itous		framed	
for'tunate		fra'mer	
for'tunately		frame'work	
for'tune		franc	
for'ty		fran'chise	
fo'rum		fran'chisement	
		frank	
for'ward		frank'ly	
for'warding			
for'wards		frank'ness	
fos'sil		fran'tic	
fos'ter		frater'nal	
fos'tered		frater'nity	
fos'tering		fraud	
fought		fraud'ulent	
foul		fraud'ulently	
fouled		fraught	
foul'ly		fray	
found		frayed	
founda'tion		freak	
found'ed		freck'le	
foun'der		free	
foun'dered		freed	
foun'dry		free'dom	
fount		free'hold	
foun'tain		free'lance	
foun'tain-head		free'ly	
four		fre'er	
four'some		freeze	
fourteen'		freez'ing	
fourteenth'		freight	
fourth		freight'age	
fowl		freight'ed	

French	friv'olously	
French'man	frock	
fren'zied	frog	
fren'zy	frol'ic	
fre'quency	*from*	
fre'quent, *adj.*	front	
frequent', *v.*	front'age	
frequent'ed	fron'tal	
frequent'ing	fron'tier	
fre'quently	fron'tispiece	
fres'co	frost	
fresh	frost'bite	
fresh'en	frost'ed	
fresh'ened	frost'y	
fresh'ening	froth	
fresh'er	frown	
fresh'est	frowned	
fresh'ly	frown'ing	
fret	froze	
fret'ful	fro'zen	
fret'ted	fru'gal	
fret'ting	frugal'ity	
fri'ar	fruit	
fric'tion	fruit'ful	
Fri'day	fruit'fulness	
fried	frui'tion	
friend	fruit'less	
friend'less	fruit'lessness	
friend'lier	frus'trate	
friend'liest	frus'trated	
friend'liness	frustra'tion	
friend'ly	fry	
friend'ship	fuch'sia	
frieze	fudge	
fright	fu'el	
fright'en	fu'gitive	
fright'ful	fulfil'	
fright'fulness	fulfilled'	
frig'id	fulfil'ment	
frigid'ity	full	
frill	full'est	
frilled	full'-length	
fringe	full'ness	
frisk	full'y	
frit'ter	ful'some	
frit'tered	fum'ble	
frivol'ity	fum'bled	
friv'olous	fume	

fumed	fur'rier
fu'migate	fur'row
fu'migated	fur'rowed
fumiga'tion	fur'ther
fun	fur'therance
func'tion	fur'thered
func'tioned	fur'thermore
fund	fur'thermost
fundamen'tal	fur'thest
	fur'tive
fu'neral	fur'tively
fune'real	fu'ry
fun'gus	fuse
fun'nel	fused
fun'niest	fu'selage
fun'ny	fu'sible
fur	fusillade'
fu'rious	fu'sion
fu'riously	fuss
furl	fuss'y
furled	fust'y
fur'long	fu'tile
fur'lough	futil'ity
fur'nace	fu'ture
fur'nish	fu'turist
fur'nisher	futuris'tic
fur'niture	futu'rity

G

gab'erdine	
ga'ble	
Gael'ic	
gadg'et	
gaffe	
gag	
gage	
gagged	
gai'ety, gay'ety	
gai'ly, gay'ly	
gain	
gained	
gain'ing	
gait	
ga'la	
gale	
gall	
gal'lant, gallant'	
gal'lantry	
gal'lery	
gal'lon	
gal'lop	
galore'	
galvan'ic	
gal'vanize	
gal'vanized	
gam'ble	
gam'bler	
gam'bling	
gam'bol	
game	
ga'mut	
gan'der	
gang	
gang'ster	
gang'way	
gaol	
gaol'er	

gap	
gape	
garage	
garb	
gar'bage	
gar'den	
gar'dener	
gar'gle	
gar'land	
gar'ment	
gar'ner	
gar'nered	
gar'nish	
garnishee'	
gar'ret	
gar'rison	
gar'rulous	
gar'ter	
gas	
gash	
gashed	
gas'-meter	
gas'olene	
gasom'eter	
gasp	
gas'tric	
gate	
gâ'teau	
gath'er	
gath'ered	
gath'ering	
gauge	
gaunt	
gaunt'let	
gauze	
gave	
gay	
gay'est	
gaze	

gazed		geriat'ric	
gazette'		germ	
gazetteer'		Ger'man	
gear		germane'	
geared		gestic'ulate	
geese		gestic'ulated	
gel'atine		ges'ture	
gem		get	
gen'der		get'ting	
gen'eral		gey'ser	
general'ity		ghast'ly	
generaliza'tion		ghost	
gen'eralize		gi'ant	
gen'eralized		gibe	
gen'erally		gid'dy	
gen'erate		gift	
gen'erated		gift'ed	
gen'erating		gigan'tic	
genera'tion		gild	
gen'erator		gild'ed	
generosity		gill (of a fish)	
gen'erous		gill (a measure)	
gen'erously		gilt	
gen'esis		gimm'ick	
ge'nial		gin	
genial'ity		gin'ger	
ge'nius		gip'sy, gyp'sy	
gen'ocide		gird	
genteel'		gird'ed	
Gen'tile		gird'er	
gen'tle		gir'dle	
gen'tleman		girl	
gen'tlemanly		girl'hood	
gen'tlemen		girth	
gen'tleness		gist	
gen'tly		give	
gen'uine		giv'en	
gen'uinely		giv'er	
geograph'ic		gives	
geograph'ical		giv'ing	
geog'raphy		glacé	
geolog'ical		gla'cial	
geol'ogist		glac'ier	
geol'ogy		glad	
geomet'ric		glad'den	
geomet'rical		glade	
geomet'rically		glad'ly	
geom'etry		glad'ness	

glam'orous		glut'ton	
glam'our,		glut'tonous	
glam'or		glyc'erine	
glance		gnash	
glanced		gnaw	
glan'cing		gnawed	
gland		go	
glare		goad	
glared		go'-ahead	
glass		goal	
glass'ful		goat	
glass'ware		gob'ble	
glass'y		gob'let	
glaze		God	
glazed		god'ly	
gleam		go'ing	
gleamed		gold	
glean		gold'en	
gleaned		gold'smith	
glee		golf	
glen		golf'er	
glib		golosh'	
glide		gone	
glim'mer		gong	
glimpse		good	
glint		good-bye'	
glis'ten		good-	
glis'tened		hu'moured	
glit'ter		goodna'ture	
glit'tered		goodna'tured	
global		good'ness	
globe		good-night'	
gloom		goods	
gloom'y		good'-sized	
glorifica'tion		goodwill'	
glo'rify		goose	
glo'rious		gore	
glo'ry		gored	
gloss		gorge	
glos'sary		gorged	
gloss'y		gor'geous	
glove		goril'la	
glow		gos'pel	
glu'cose		gos'sip	
glue		got	
glu'ey		Goth'ic	
glum		gouge	
glut			

gov'ern	
gov'erned	
gov'erning	
gov'ernment	
governmen'tal	
gov'ernor	
gov'ernorship	
gown	
grab	
grace	
grace'ful	
grace'fully	
gra'cious	
gra'ciously	
grada'tion	
grade	
gra'ded	
gra'dient	
gra'ding	
grad'ual	
grad'ually	
grad'uate	
grad'uated	
gradua'tion	
graffi'ti	
graft	
graft'ed	
graft'er	
graft'ing	
grain	
gram'mar	
gramma'rian	
grammat'ical	
gram'ophone	
gran'ary	
grand	
grand'- daughter	
grand'est	
gran'deur	
grand'father	
grand'mother	
grand'parent	
grand'son	
grange	
gran'ite	
grant	
grant'ed	

gran'ulate	
gran'ulated	
grape	
graph'ic	
graph'ically	
graph'ite	
grap'ple	
grap'pled	
grap'pling	
grasp	
grasped	
grasp'ing	
grass	
grass'y	
grate	
grate'ful	
gratifica'tion	
grat'ified	
grat'ify	
gra'tis	
grat'itude	
gratu'itous	
gratu'ity	
grave	
grav'el	
grave'ly	
gravita'tion	
grav'ity	
gra'vy	
gray, grey	
graze	
grazed	
grease	
greas'y	
great	
great'er	
great'est	
great'ly	
great'ness	
Gre'cian	
greed	
greed'ily	
greed'y	
Greek	
green	
green'house	
greet	

greet'ed
greet'ing
grega'rious
grew
grey'hound
grid
grief
griev'ance
grieve
grieved
griev'ous
griev'ously
grill, grille
grilled
grim
grimace'
grime
grin
grinned
grin'ning
grind
grind'er
grind'ing
grip
gripe
grit
groan
groaned
groan'ing
gro'cer
gro'cery
groom
groove
grooved
grope
gross
grotesque'
ground
ground'less
ground'-nut
ground'-plan
ground'work
group
grouped
group'ing
grove
grov'el
grow

grow'er
growl
growled
grown
growth
grub
grudge
grudg'ingly
grue'some
gruff
gruff'ly
grum'ble
grum'bled
grunt
grun'ted
guarantee'
guaranteed'
guarantee'ing
guarantor'
guaranty
guard
guard'ed
guard'ian
guard'ianship
guard'ing
guess
guessed
guess'work
guest
guid'ance
guide
guild
guild'hall
guile
guillotine'
guilt
guilt'y
guin'ea
guise
guitar'
gulf
gull
gulled
gul'let
gul'lible
gulp
gum
gummed

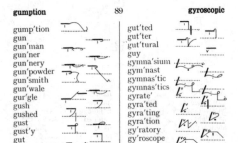

gump'tion
gun
gun'man
gun'ner
gun'nery
gun'powder
gun'smith
gun'wale
gur'gle
gush
gushed
gust
gust'y
gut
gut'ta-per'cha

gut'ted
gut'ter
gut'tural
guy
gymna'sium
gym'nast
gymnas'tic
gymnas'tics
gyrate'
gyra'ted
gyra'ting
gyra'tion
gy'ratory
gy'roscope
gyroscop'ic

H

hab'it
hab'itable
habita'tion
habit'ual
habit'uate
hack
hack'ney
hack'neyed
had
haem'orrhage,
   hem'orrhage
hag
hag'gard
hag'gle
hail
hailed
hair
hair'dresser
hair'y
hale
half
half'-caste
half-heart'ed
half-nelson
half'-price
hall
hall'mark
hal'low
halt
halt'ed
hal'ter
halve
halved
ham
ham'hand'ed
ham'let
ham'mer
ham'mered
ham'mock
ham'per

ham'pered
hand
hand'bag
hand'ed
hand'ful
hand'icap
hand'icraft
hand'ing
hand'iwork
hand'kerchief
hand'le
hand'led
hand'ling
hand'-made
hand'out
hand'some
hand'work
hand'writing
hand'y
hang
hang'ar
hanged
hang'er
hang'over
hank'er
haphaz'ard
hap'pen
hap'pened
hap'pening
hap'pier
hap'piest
hap'pily
hap'piness
hap'py
harangue'
harangued'
har'ass
har'bour,
   har'bor

90

hard	haugh'ty
hard'board	haul
hard'en	haul'age
hard'ened	hauled
hard'er	haunt
hard'est	haunt'ed
hard'-hearted	Havan'a
hard'ly	*have*
hard'ness	ha'ven
hard'ship	*hav'ing*
hard'ware	hav'oc
hard'y	hawk
hare	hawk'er
harm	haw'thorn
harmed	hay
harm'ful	hay'stack
harm'less	haz'ard
harmon'ics	haz'ardous
harmo'nious	haze
har'monize	ha'zel
har'mony	ha'ziness
har'ness	ha'zy
harp	he
harpoon'	head
har'row	head'ache
har'rowed	head'light
har'rowing	head'line
harsh	head'long
harsh'ly	headmast'er
har'vest	
har'vested	head'quart'ers
har'vesting	head'stone
has	
hash	head'strong
haste	head'way
ha'sten	heal
ha'stened	healed
ha'stily	health
ha'sty	health'ful
hat	health'ier
hatch	health'iest
hatched	health'y
hatch'et	heap
hatch'ing	hear
hate	heard
hate'ful	hear'er
hate'fully	hear'ing
ha'tred	hear'say
	heart

heart'en	hen
heart'ening	hence
heart'felt	henceforth'
hearth	
heart'ily	hencefor'ward
heart'y	her
heat	her'ald
heat'ed	her'alded
heat'er	her'aldry
heath	herb
heath'en	Hercu'lean
heat'ing	herd
heave	herd'ed
heav'en	here
heav'enly	hereaf'ter
heav'ily	hereby'
heav'y	hered'itary
Hebra'ic	hered'ity
He'brew	here*in*'
heck'le	here*of*'
hec'tic	here*on*'
hedge	here*to*'
heed	heretofore'
heed'ful	hereun'der
heed'less	here*with*'
heel	her'itage
heif'er	her'mit
height	he'ro
height'en	hero'ic
hei'nous	he'roin
heir	her'oine
heir'ess	her'oism
held	her'ring
hel'icopter	hers
hel'iport	herself'
hell	hes'itancy
helm	hes'itant
helm'et	hes'itate
help	hes'itated
help'er	hes'itating
help'ful	hes'itatingly
help'fulness	hesita'tion
help'less	hew
help'lessness	hewed
hem	hewn
hem'isphere	hex'agon
hemp	hia'tus
hemp'en	hid

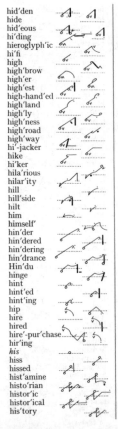

hid'den	hit
hide	hitch
hid'eous	hith'er
hi'ding	hither*to'*
hieroglyph'ic	hive
hi'fi	hoard
high	hoard'ed
high'brow	hoard'er
high'er	hoard'ing
high'est	hoarse
high-hand'ed	hoarse'ly
high'land	hoarse'ness
high'ly	hoax
high'ness	hoaxed
high'road	hob'ble
high'way	hob'by
hi'-jacker	hock'ey
hike	hod
hi'ker	hoe
hila'rious	hoed
hilar'ity	loes
hill	hog
hill'side	hoist
hilt	hoist'ed
him	hoist'ing
himself'	hold
hin'der	hold'er
hin'dered	hold'ing
hin'dering	hold'up
hin'drance	hole
Hin'du	hol'iday
hinge	ho'liness
hint	hol'low
hint'ed	hol'lowed
hint'ing	ho'ly
hip	hom'age
hire	home
hired	home'coming
hire'-pur'chase	home'less
hir'ing	home'ly
his	home'sick
hiss	home'stead
hissed	home'ward
hist'amine	home'work
histo'rian	hom'icide
histor'ic	hom'ily
histor'ical	homoge'neous
his'tory	hom'onym

hon′est	host
hon′estly	hos′tage
hon′esty	hos′tel
hon′ey	host′ess
hon′eymoon	hos′tile
honora′rium	hostil′ity
hon′orary	hot
hon′our,	hotel′
hon′or	hot′house
hon′ourable	hot′ter
hon′oured	hot′test
hon′ours	hound
hood	*hour*
hood′wink	*hour′ly*
hoof	house
hook	house′hold
hop	house′holder
hope	house′keeper
hope′ful	house′keeping
hope′fulness	house′work
hope′less	hous′ing
hope′lessness	hov′el
hop′ing	hov′er
horde	hov′ering
hori′zon	*how*
horizon′tal	howev′er
hor′mone	howl
horn	howled
hor′rible	howsoev′er
hor′rid	hub
hor′rified	hud′dle
hor′rify	hue
hor′ror	huff
hors-d′oeuv′res	hug
horse	huge
horse′back	hulk
Horse′ Guards	hull
horse′hair	hum
horse′man	hu′man
horse′manship	humane′
horse′-power	humane′ly
hort′iculture	humanis′tic
	humanita′rian
hose	human′ity
ho′siery	hu′manly
hos′pitable	hum′ble
hos′pital	hum′bler
hospital′ity	hum′blest

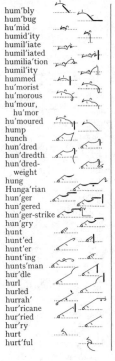

hum'bly
hum'bug
hu'mid
humid'ity
humil'iate
humil'iated
humilia'tion
humil'ity
hummed
hu'morist
hu'morous
hu'mour,
  hu'mor
hu'moured
hump
hunch
hun'dred
hun'dredth
hun'dred-
  weight
hung
Hunga'rian
hun'ger
hun'gered
hun'ger-strike
hun'gry
hunt
hunt'ed
hunt'er
hunt'ing
hunts'man
hur'dle
hurl
hurled
hurrah'
hur'ricane
hur'ried
hur'ry
hurt
hurt'ful

hus'band
hus'banded
hus'banding
hush
hushed
husk
husk'ily
husk'iness
husk'y
hus'tle
hus'tled
hus'tler
hut
hy'brid
hy'drant
hydraul'ic
hy'drofoil
hy'drogen
hy'drophone
hydropon'ics
hy'giene
hygien'ic
hymn
hyper'bole
hypercrit'ical
hyperson'ic
hy'phen
hypno'sis
hyp'notism
hyp'notize
hypoc'risy
hyp'ocrite
hypocrit'ical
hypothet'ical
hysterec'tomy
hyste'ria
hyster'ical
hyster'ics
hythe

I

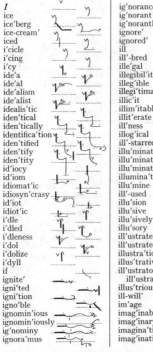

I	
ice	
ice'berg	
ice-cream'	
iced	
i'cicle	
i'cing	
i'cy	
ide'a	
ide'al	
ide'alism	
ide'alist	
idealis'tic	
iden'tical	
iden'tically	
identifica'tion	
iden'tified	
iden'tify	
iden'tity	
id'iocy	
id'iom	
idiomat'ic	
idiosyn'crasy	
id'iot	
idiot'ic	
i'dle	
i'dled	
i'dleness	
i'dol	
i'dolize	
i'dyll	
if	
ignite'	
igni'ted	
igni'tion	
igno'ble	
ignomin'ious	
ignomin'iously	
ig'nominy	
ignora'mus	

ig'norance	
ig'norant	
ig'norantly	
ignore'	
ignored'	
ill	
ill'-bred	
ille'gal	
illegibil'ity	
illeg'ible	
illegi'timate	
illic'it	
illim'itable	
illit'erate	
ill'ness	
illog'ical	
ill'-starred'	
illu'minate	
illu'minated	
illu'minating	
illumina'tion	
illu'mine	
ill'-used	
illu'sion	
illu'sive	
illu'sively	
illu'sory	
ill'ustrate	
ill'ustrated	
illustra'tion	
illus'trative	
ill'ustrator,	
ill'ustrater	
illus'trious	
ill-will'	
im'age	
imag'inable	
imag'inary	
imagina'tion	
imag'inative	

96

imag'ine	
imag'ined	
imag'ining	
im'becile	
imbecil'ity	
imbibe'	
imbibed'	
imbue'	
imbued'	
im'itate	
im'itated	
im'itating	
imita'tion	
im'itative	
im'itator	
immac'ulate	
immate'rial	
immature'	
immeas'urable	
imme'diate	
imme'diately	
immemo'rial	
immense'	
immense'ly	
immen'sity	
immerse'	
immer'sion	
im'migrant	
im'migrate	
immigra'tion	
im'minence	
im'minent	
immo'bile	
immod'erate	
immod'erately	
immod'est	
immod'estly	
immor'al	
immoral'ity	
immor'tal	
immortal'ity	
immor'talize	
immov'able	
immune'	
immu'nity	
immu'table	
imp	

{im'pact, *n.*	
{impact', *v.*	
impair'	
impaired'	
impart'	
impart'ed	
impar'tial	
impartial'ity	
impas'sable	
impas'sioned	
impas'sive	
impa'tience	
impa'tient	
impa'tiently	
impeach'	
impeach'ment	
impecu'nious	
impede'	
imped'iment	
impel'	
impelled'	
impend'	
impend'ing	
impen'etrable	
impen'itent	
imper'ative	
imper'atively	
impercep'tible	
imper'fect	
imperfec'tion	
imper'fectly	
imper'il	
impe'rious	
imper'ishable	
imper'sonal	
imper'sonate	
impersona'tion	
imper'tinence	
imper'tinent	
imper'tinently	
imperturb'able	
imper'vious	
impet'uous	
impet'uously	
im'petus	
impinge'	
im'pious	

impla'cable	
implant'	
implant'ed	
implement	
im'plicate	
implica'tion	
implic'it	
implied'	
implore'	
implored'	
imply'	
impolite'	
im'port, *n.*	
import', *v.*	
impor'tance	
impor'tant	
importa'tion	
import'ed	
import'er	
impor'tunate	
importune'	
impose'	
imposi'tion	
impossibil'ity	
impos'sible	
im'post	
impos'tor	
impos'ture	
im'potence	
im'potency	
im'potent	
im'potently	
impound'	
impound'ed	
impov'erish	
impov'erished	
impov'erish- ment	
imprac'tic- able	
impreca'tion	
impreg'nable	
im'press, *n.*	
impress', *v.*	
impres'sion	
impres'sion- able	
impress'ive	

impress'ively	
im'print, *n.*	
imprint', *v.*	
imprint'ed	
impris'on	
impris'oned	
impris'onment	
improbabil'- ity	
improb'able	
improb'ably	
impromp'tu	
improp'er	
improp'erly	
impropri'ety	
improve'	
improved'	
improve'- ment	
improv'idence	
improv'ident	
improv'idently	
improv'ing	
improviza'tion	
improvize'	
impru'dence	
impru'dent	
impru'dently	
im'pudence	
im'pudent	
im'pudently	
impugn'	
impugned'	
im'pulse	
impul'sive	
impul'sively	
impu'nity	
impure'	
impu'rity	
imputa'tion	
impute'	
impu'ted	
impu'ting	
in	
inabil'ity	
inaccess'ible	
inac'curacy	
inac'curate	

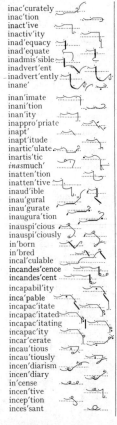

inac'curately
inac'tion
inact'ive
inactiv'ity
inad'equacy
inad'equate
inadmis'sible
inadvert'ent
inadvert'ently
inane'

inan'imate
inani'tion
inan'ity
inappro'priate
inapt'
inapt'itude
inartic'ulate
inartis'tic
*inas*much'
inatten'tion
inatten'tive
inaud'ible
inau'gural
inau'gurate
inaugura'tion
inauspi'cious
inauspi'ciously
in'born
in'bred
incal'culable
incandes'cence
incandes'cent
incapabil'ity
inca'pable
incapac'itate
incapac'itated
incapac'itating
incapac'ity
incar'cerate
incau'tious
incau'tiously
incen'diarism
incen'diary
in'cense
incen'tive
incep'tion
inces'sant

inces'santly
inch
in'cidence
in'cident
inciden'tal
incin'erate
incin'erator
incip'ient
inci'sion
inci'sive
incite'
incite'ment
incivil'ity
inclem'ency
inclem'ent
inclina'tion
incline'
inclined'
inclose'
inclo'sure
include'
inclu'ded
inclu'ding
inclu'sion
inclu'sive
incoher'ency
incoher'ent
in'come
in'coming
incom'parable
incompati-
  bil'ity
incompat'ible
incom'petence
incom'petent
incom'petently
incomplete'
incomprehen'-
  sible
inconceiv'able
inconclu'sive
inconclu'sively
incongru'ity
incon'gruous
incon'sequent
inconsequen'-
  tial
inconsid'erable

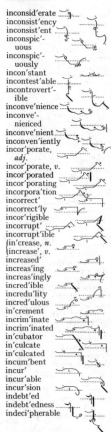

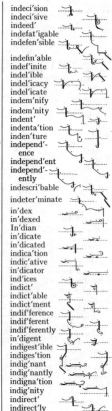

inconsid'erate
inconsist'ency
inconsist'ent
inconspic'-
  uous
inconspic'-
  uously
incon'stant
incontest'able
incontrovert'-
  ible
inconve'nience
inconve'-
  nienced
inconve'nient
inconven'iently
incor'porate, adj.
incor'porate, v.
incor'porated
incor'porating
incorpora'tion
incorrect'
incorrect'ly
incor'rigible
incorrupt'
incorrupt'ible
in'crease, n.
increase', v.
increased'
increas'ing
increas'ingly
incred'ible
incredu'lity
incred'ulous
in'crement
incrim'inate
incrim'inated
in'cubator
in'culcate
in'culcated
incum'bent
incur'
incur'able
incur'sion
indebt'ed
indebt'edness
indeci'pherable

indeci'sion
indeci'sive
indeed'
indefat'igable
indefen'sible
indefin'able
indef'inite
indel'ible
indel'icacy
indel'icate
indem'nify
indem'nity
indent'
indenta'tion
inden'ture
independ'-
  ence
independ'ent
independ'-
  ently
indescri'bable
indeter'minate
in'dex
in'dexed
In'dian
in'dicate
in'dicated
indica'tion
indic'ative
in'dicator
ind'ices
indict'
indict'able
indict'ment
indif'ference
indif'ferent
indif'ferently
in'digent
indigest'ible
indiges'tion
indig'nant
indig'nantly
indigna'tion
indig'nity
indirect'
indirect'ly

indiscreet'	
indiscre'tion	
indiscrim'inate	
indiscrim'in-ately	
indispen'-sable	
indispen'-sably	
indispose'	
indisposed'	
indisposi'tion	
indispu'table	
indistinct'	
indistin'guish-able	
indite'	
individ'ual	
individ'ualist	
individual'ity	
individ'ually	
indivis'ible	
in'dolence	
in'dolent	
in'dolently	
indom'itable	
in'door	
indorse'	
indorse'ment	
indors'er	
indu'bitable	
induce'	
induced'	
induce'ment	
induct'	
induc'tion	
indulge'	
indul'gence	
indul'gent	
indul'gently	
indul'ging	
indus'trial	
indus'trialist	
industrial-iza'tion	
indus'trious	
in'dustry	
inebria'tion	

ined'ible	
ineffec'tual	
ineffi'ciency	
ineffi'cient	
ineffi'ciently	
inel'egant	
inel'igible	
inequal'ity	
inerad'icable	
inert'	
iner'tia	
ines'timable	
inev'itable	
inexact'	
inexcus'able	
inexhaust'ible	
inex'orable	
inexpe'dient	
inexpen'sive	
inexpe'rience	
inex'plicable	
inex'tricable	
infallibil'ity	
infal'lible	
in'famous	
in'famy	
in'fancy	
in'fant	
in'fantile	
in'fantry	
infat'uate	
infatua'tion	
infect'	
infected'	
infec'tion	
infec'tious	
infer'	
in'ference	
infe'rior	
inferior'ity	
infer'nal	
infer'no	
inferred'	
infest'	
infest'ed	
in'fidel	

infidel'ity	infu'riated
in'finite	infuse'
in'finitely	infused'
	inge'nious
infinites'imal	inge'niously
	ingenu'ity
infin'ity	ingen'uous
infirm'	ingen'uously
infir'mary	inglo'rious
infir'mity	in'got
inflame'	ingrain'
inflamed'	in'grate
inflammabil'-	ingra'tiate
ity	ingra'tiated
inflam'mable	ingra'tiating
inflamma'tion	ingrat'itude
inflate'	ingre'dient
infla'ted	inhab'it
infla'ting	inhab'itable
infla'tion	inhab'itant
(inflec'tion	inhab'ited
(inflex'ion	inhala'tion
inflexibil'ity	inhale'
inflex'ible	inhaled'
inflict'	inher'ent
inflict'ed	inher'it
inflic'tion	inher'itance
in'fluence	inher'ited
in'fluenced	inhibi'tion
in'fluencing	inhos'pitable
influen'tial	inhu'man
influen'tially	inim'ical
influen'za	inim'itable
in'flux	iniq'uitous
inform'	iniq'uity
inform'al	ini'tial
informal'ity	ini'tialled,
inform'ant	ini'tialed
informa'tion	ini'tiate
inform'ative	ini'tiated
informed'	initia'tion
inform'er	ini'tiative
inform'ing	inject'
infra'-red	inject'ed
infre'quent	injec'tion
infre'quently	injudi'cious
infringe'	injudi'ciously
infringe'ment	injunc'tion
infu'riate	

in'jure	inscru'table
in'jured	in'sect
inju'rious	insecure'
inju'riously	insecu'rity
in'jury	insensibil'ity
injus'tice	insen'sible
ink	insen'sibly
inlaid	insep'arable
in'land	insert'
in'let	insert'ed
in'mate	inser'tion
in'most	(in'set, n.
inn	(inset', v.
innate'	in'side
in'ner	insid'ious
in'nermost	in'sight
in'nocence	insig'nia
in'nocent	insignif'icance
in'nocently	insignif'icant
innoc'uous	insincere'
innova'tion	insincere'ly
innuen'do	insincer'ity
innu'merable	insin'uate
inoc'ulate	insin'uated
inoc'ulated	insin'uating
inocula'tion	insinua'tion
inopportune'	insip'id
inopportune'ly	insist'
inor'dinate	insist'ed
inorgan'ic	insist'ence
in'-patient	insist'ent
in'put	insist'ently
in'quest	insobri'ety
inquire'	in'solence
inquired'	in'solent
inquir'er	in'solently
inquir'y	insol'uble
inquis'itive	insolv'ency
inquis'itively	insolv'ent
in'road	insom'nia
insane'	inspect'
insan'itary	inspect'ed
insan'ity	inspect'ing
insa'tiable	inspec'tion
inscribe'	inspec'tor
inscribed'	inspira'tion
inscri'bing	inspire'
inscrip'tion	inspired'

inspir'ing
instabil'ity
install'
installa'tion
installed'
instal'ment
in'stance
in'stanced
in'stant
instanta'neous
instanta'ne-
ously
in'stantly
instead'
in'step
in'stigate
in'stigated
in'stigator
instil', instill'
in'stinct
instinc'tive
instinc'tively
in'stitute
in'stituted
institu'tion
instruct'
instruct'ed
instruc'tion
instruc'tive
instruct'or
in'strument
instrumen'tal
insubor'dinate
insubordina'-
tion
insuf'ferable
insuffi'ciency
insuffi'cient
insuffi'ciently
in'sular
in'sulate
in'sulated
insula'tion
in'sulator
in'sulin
{in'sult, n.
{insult', v.
insult'ed

insult'ing
insu'perable
insupport'able
insur'able
insur'ance
insure'
insured'
insur'gent
insurmount'-
able
insurrec'tion
intact'
intan'gible
in'tegral
in'tegrate
integ'rity
in'tellect
intellec'tual
intel'ligence
intel'ligent
intel'ligently
intelligent'sia
intel'ligible
intel'ligibly
intem'perance
intem'perate
intem'perately
intend'
intend'ed
intense'
intense'ly
inten'sify
inten'sity
inten'sive
intent'
inten'tion
inten'tional
intent'ly
inter'
intercede'
intercept'
intercept'ed
{in'terchange,
{ n.
{interchange'
{ v.

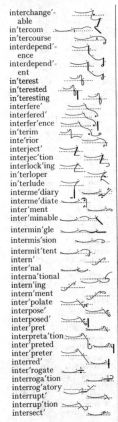

interchange'-
  able
in'tercom
in'tercourse
interdepend'-
  ence
interdepend'-
  ent
in'terest
in'terested
in'teresting
interfere'
interfered'
interfer'ence
in'terim
inte'rior
interject'
interjec'tion
interlock'ing
in'terloper
in'terlude
interme'diary
interme'diate
inter'ment
inter'minable

intermin'gle
intermis'sion
intermit'tent
intern'
inter'nal
interna'tional
intern'ing
intern'ment
inter'polate
interpose'
interposed'
inter'pret
interpreta'tion
inter'preted
inter'preter
interred'
inter'rogate
interroga'tion
interrog'atory
interrupt'
interrup'tion
intersect'

intersect'ed
intersec'tion
intersperse'
interspersed'
intertwine'
in'terval
intervene'
interven'tion
in'terview
interwov'en
intes'tate
intes'tine
in'timacy
in'timate, n.,
  adj.
in'timate, v.
in'timately
in'timating
intima'tion
intim'idate
intim'idated
intimida'tion
in'to

intol'erable
intol'erance
intol'erant
intona'tion
intox'icant
intox'icate
intox'icated
intoxica'tion
intrep'id
in'tricacy
in'tricate
intrigue'
intrin'sic

intrin'sically
introduce'
introduced'
introduc'tion
introduc'tory
introspec'tion
introspec'tive
in'trovert
intrude'
intru'ded
intru'sion

intui′tion	invi′ted
intu′itive	invoca′tion
intu′itively	in′voice
in′undate	in′voiced
in′undated	invoke′
inunda′tion	invoked′
inure′	invol′untary
invade′	involve′
in′valid	involved′
inval′id	invul′nerable
inval′idate	
inval′uable	in′ward
inva′riable	in′wardly
inva′sion	i′odine
invec′tive	i′onize
inveigh′	ion′osphere
invei′gle	io′ta
invent′	iras′cible
invent′ed	irate′
inven′tion	ire
invent′ive	I′rish
invent′or	irk′some
in′ventory	i′ron
inverse′	iron′ic
inver′sion	iron′ical
invert′	i′ronmonger
invert′ed	i′rony
invest′	irra′tional
invest′ed	irrecov′erable
inves′tigate	irredeem′able
inves′tigated	
investiga′tion	irredu′cible
inves′tigator	irrefu′table
invest′ing	
invest′ment	irreg′ular
invest′or	irregular′ity
invet′erate	irrel′evancy
invid′ious	irrel′evant
invigila′tion	irreme′diable
invig′orate	irremov′able
invig′orated	irrep′arable
invin′cible	irrepres′sible
invi′olable	irreproach′able
	irresist′ible
invi′olate	irres′olute
invis′ible	irrespec′tive
invita′tion	irrespec′tively
invite′	

irrespon-sibil'ity	isola'tion
irrespon'sible	isola'tionist
irretriev'able	is'otope
irrev'erent	is'sue
	is'sued
irrev'erently	is'suing
irrev'ocable	*it*
ir'rigate	Ital'ian
ir'rigated	ital'ic
irriga'tion	ital'ics
ir'ritable	ital'icize
ir'ritate	itch
ir'ritated	i'tem
irrita'tion	i'temize
is	itin'erant
is'land	itin'erary
is'lander	itin'erate
isle	*its*
i'solate	*itself'*
i'solating	i'vory
	i'vy

J

jack		
jack'et		
jack'pot		
Jacobe'an		
jade		
ja'ded		
jag		
jagged		
jag'ged		
jail		
jail'er		
jail'or		
jam		
jamb		
jammed		
jan'gle		
jan'gled		
jan'itor		
Jan'uary		
Japan'		
Japanese'		
jar		
jar'gon		
jar'ring		
jar'ringly		
jaun'dice		
jaunt		
jaun'tily		
jaw		
jay'wa'lker		
jeal'ous		
jeal'ousy		
jeer		
jeered		
jel'ly		
jeop'ardize		
jeop'ardy		
jerk		
jerked		
jer'ry		

jer'sey		
jest		
jest'ed		
jest'er		
jest'ing		
jest'ingly		
jet		
jet'sam		
jet'tison		
jet'ty		
Jew		
jew'el		
jew'eller, jew'eler		
jew'ellery		
jew'elry		
Jew'ess		
Jew'ish		
jibe		
jig'saw		
jin'gle		
jitt'ery		
job		
job'ber		
job'bery		
jock'ey		
jocose'		
joc'ular		
jog		
join		
join'er		
join'ing		
joint		
joint'ed		
joint'ly		
joke		
jo'kingly		
jol'lity		
jol'ly		
jolt		

jos'tle	juice
jos'tled	juke'-box
jot	July'
jot'ted	jum'ble
jot'ting	jum'bo
jour'nal	jump
journalese'	jumped
jour'nalism	jump'er
jour'nalist	junc'tion
journalis'tic	junc'ture
jour'ney	June
jour'neyed	jun'gle
jo'vial	ju'nior
joviral'ity	junk
joy	jurisdic'tion
joy'ful	ju'rist
joy'ous	ju'ror
joy'ously	ju'ry
ju'bilant	ju'ryman
jubila'tion	just
ju'bilee	jus'tice
judge	jus'tifiable
judged	justifica'tion
judg'ing	jus'tified
judg'ment	jus'tify
ju'dicature	just'ly
judi'cial	just'ness
judi'cious	jut
judi'ciously	jut'ted
jug	jut'ting
jug'gle	ju'venile
jug'gler	juxtaposi'tion
ju'gular	

K

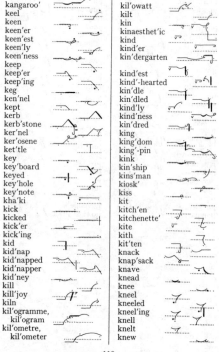

kangaroo'
keel
keen
keen'er
keen'est
keen'ly
keen'ness
keep
keep'er
keep'ing
keg
ken'nel
kept
kerb
kerb'stone
ker'nel
ker'osene
ket'tle
key
key'board
keyed
key'hole
key'note
kha'ki
kick
kicked
kick'er
kick'ing
kid
kid'nap
kid'napped
kid'napper
kid'ney
kill
kill'joy
kiln
kil'ogramme,
    kil'ogram
kil'ometre,
    kil'ometer

kil'owatt
kilt
kin
kinaesthet'ic
kind
kind'er
kin'dergarten
kind'est
kind'-hearted
kin'dle
kin'dled
kind'ly
kind'ness
kin'dred
king
king'dom
king'-pin
kink
kin'ship
kins'man
kiosk'
kiss
kit
kitch'en
kitchenette'
kite
kith
kit'ten
knack
knap'sack
knave
knead
knee
kneel
kneeled
kneel'ing
knell
knelt
knew

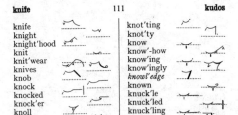

knife	knot'ting
knight	knot'ty
knight'hood	know'-how
knit	know'ing
knit'wear	know'ingly
knives	*knowl'edge*
knob	known
knock	knuck'le
knocked	knuck'led
knock'er	knuck'ling
knoll	ko'dak
knot	ku'dos
knot'ted	

L

la'bel
la'belled,
   la'beled
la'belling,
   la'beling
lab'oratory
labo'rious
labo'riously
la'bour, la'bor
la'bourer

labur'num
lab'yrinth
lace
lac'erate
lac'erated
lacera'tion
lach'rymose
la'cing
lack
lackadai'sical
lacked
lacon'ic
lac'quer,
   lack'er
lac'tate
lad
lad'der
la'den
la'dle
la'dy
la'dyship
lag
la'ger
lag'gard
lagged
laid
lain
lair
la'ity

lake
lamb
lam'bent
lame
lamed
lament'
lam'entable
lamenta'tion
lament'ed
lament'ing
lam'ia
lam'inate
lamp
lance
lan'cet
land
land'ed
land'holder
land'ing
land'lady
land'lord
land'mark
land'owner
land'-rover
land'scape
land'slide
lane
lan'guage
lan'guid
lan'guish
lan'gour
lank'y
lan'tern
lap
lapel'
lapse
lapsed
laps'ing
lar'ceny

112

larch	launched
lard	launch'ing
lard'er	laun'dry
large	lau'reate
large'ly	lau'rel
larg'er	la'va
larg'est	lav'atory
lark	lav'ender
lar'va	lav'ish
lar'vae	lav'ished
laryngi'tis	lav'ishly
	law
lar'ynx	law'ful
	law'fully
las'car	law'fulness
la'ser	law'less
lash	law'lessness
lashed	lawn
lash'ing	law'suit
lass	law'yer
las'situde	lax
last	lax'ative
last'ed	lax'ity
last'ing	lay
last'ingly	lay'by
last'ly	lay'er
latch	lay'ing
late	lay'man
late'ly	lay'out
la'tent	laze
la'ter	la'zier
lat'eral	la'zily
la'test	la'ziness
lath	la'zy
lathe	lea
lath'er	lead (a metal)
Lat'in	lead (to conduct)
lat'itude	
lat'ter	lead'en
lat'terly	lead'er
at'tice	lead'ership
ïaud	lead'ing
laud'able	leaf
laud'anum	leaf'let
laud'atory	leaf'y
laugh	league
laugh'ingly	leagued
laugh'ter	leak
launch	

leak'age	
leak'y	
lean	
leaned	
lean'est	
lean'ing	
leant	
leap	
leaped	
leap'ing	
leapt	
learn	
learned	
learn'ed	
learn'er	
learn'ing	
learnt	
lease	
lease'hold	
lease'holder	
leash	
leashed	
leas'ing	
least	
leath'er	
leave	
leav'en	
lec'ture	
lec'tured	
lec'turer	
lec'turing	
led	
ledge	
ledg'er	
leek	
leer	
leered	
leer'ing	
leer'ingly	
lee'ward	
lee'way	
left	
left'-handed	
leg	
leg'acy	
le'gal	
legal'ity	

le'galize	
le'gally	
legatee'	
lega'tion	
leg'end	
leg'endary	
leg'erdemain	
legibil'ity	
leg'ible	
le'gion	
leg'islate	
leg'islated	
legisla'tion	
leg'islative	
leg'islator	
leg'islature	
legit'imacy	
legit'imate, *adj.*	
legitimate', *v.*	
lei'sure	
lei'surely	
lem'on	
lemonade'	
lend	
lend'er	
lend'ing	
length	
length'en	
length'ening	
length'wise	
length'y	
le'nience	
le'niency	
le'nient	
le'niently	
lens	
Lent, lent	
leop'ard	
lep'er	
lep'rosy	
les'bian	
less	
lessee'	
les'sen	
les'sened	
les'sening	
les'ser	

les'son		lick	
lessor'		licked	
lest		lid	
let		lid'o	
le'thal		lie	
lethar'gic		lied	
leth'argy		li'en	
let'ter		lieu	
let'terbox		lieuten'ant	
let'terhead		life	
let'terpress		life'boat	
let'ting		life'guard	
let'tuce		life'-insurance	
leukaem'ia		life'less	
lev'ee		life'-preserver	
lev'el		lifesav'er	
lev'elled,		life'-size	
lev'eled		life'time	
lev'elling,		lift	
lev'eling		lift'ed	
le'ver		lift'ing	
le'verage		lig'ament	
levi'athan		lig'ature	
lev'ity		light	
lev'y		light'ed	
liabil'ity		light'ening	
li'able		light'er	
liais'on-officer		light'erage	
li'ar		light'hearted	
li'bel		light'house	
li'bellous,		light'ing	
li'belous		light'ning	
lib'eral		like	
liberal'ity		like'able	
lib'erally		liked	
lib'erate		like'lihood	
lib'erated		like'ly	
lib'erating		li'ken	
libera'tion		li'kened	
lib'erty		like'ness	
libra'rian		like'wise	
li'brary		li'lac	
(li'cence, _n._		lil'y	
(li'cense, _v._		limb	
li'censed		lim'ber	
licensee'		lim'bo	
licen'tious		lime	
li'chen			

lime'light		liq'uorice,
lime'stone		lic'orice
lime'water		lisp
lim'it		list
limita'tion		list'ed
lim'ited		lis'ten
lim'iting		lis'tened
limp		lis'tener
limped		list'ing
lim'pet		list'less
lim'pid		list'lessly
limp'ing		list'lessness
line		lit
lin'eage		lit'any
lin'eal		lit'eral
lineal'ity		lit'erally
lin'eament		lit'erary
lin'ear		lit'erature
lined		lithe
lin'en		lithog'rapher
li'ner		lithograph'ic
lin'ger		lithog'raphy
lin'gered		lit'igant
lin'gerie		lit'igate
lin'guist		litiga'tion
linguis'tic		lit'ter
lin'iment		lit'tered
li'ning		lit'tle
link		lit'urgy
lino'leum		live, v.
li'notype		live, a.
lin'seed		lived
lint		live'lihood
li'on		live'long
li'oness		live'ly
lip		liv'er
lip'stick		liv'ery
liq'uefy		lives
liqueur'		lives, pl.
liq'uid		live'stock
liq'uidate		liv'id
liq'uidated		load
liq'uidating		load'ed
liquida'tion		load'ing
liq'uidator		loaf
liq'uidize		loaf'er
liq'uor		loaf'ing
		loam

loan	lone'some
loan'ing	long
loath, loth	longed
loathe	long'er, *n.*
loath'some	lon'ger, *adj.*
loaves	lon'gest
lob'by	longev'ity
lob'ster	long'hand
lo'cal	lon'gitude
local'ity	longitu'dinal
lo'calize	long'lived
lo'cally	
locate'	long'suffering
loca'ted	loo'fah
loca'ting	look
loca'tion	looked
loch	look'ing
lock	look'out
locked	loom
lock'er	loomed
lock'et	loom'ing
lock'out	loop
lock'smith	loop'hole
lo'como'tion	loose
lo'comotive	loosed
lo'cum-te'nens	loose'ly
lo'cust	loos'en
lode	loos'ened
lodge	loos'er
lodged	loqua'cious
lodg'ing	loquac'ity
loft	lord
loft'ier	lord'ship
loft'iest	lore
loft'ily	lor'ry
loft'y	lose
log	los'er
log'ic	los'ing
log'ical	loss
logi'cian	lost
loin	lot
loi'ter	lo'tion
loi'tered	lot'tery
loll	loud
lolled	loud'er
lone	loud'speaker
lone'liness	lounge
lone'ly	lov'able

love	
love'lier	
love'liest	
love'liness	
love'ly	
lov'er	
low	
low'er	
low'ered	
low'est	
low'land	
low'ly	
loy'al	
loy'alty	
loz'enge	
lu'bricant	
lu'bricate	
lu'bricated	
lubrica'tion	
lu'bricator	
lu'cid	
lucid'ity	
luck	
luck'ier	
luck'iest	
luck'y	
lu'crative	
lu'dicrous	
lug'gage	
luke'warm	
lull	
lull'aby	
lulled	

lull'ing	
lumba'go	
lum'ber	
lu'minous	
lump	
lu'nacy	
lu'nar	
lu'natic	
lunch	
lunch'eon	
lung	
lunge	
lurch	
lure	
lured	
lu'rid	
lurk	
lus'cious	
lus'tre	
lus'trous	
lust'y	
lute	
luxu'riance	
luxu'riant	
luxu'rious	
luxu'riously	
lux'ury	
ly'ing	
lynch	
lynx	
lyr'ic	
lyr'ical	

M

maca'bre

macad'amize

mace

machina'tion

machine'

machin'ery

machine'-tool

machin'ist

mack'erel

mack'intosh

macrobiot'ics

mac'ron

mad

mad'am

mad'den

mad'dening

made

maes'tro

magazine'

mag'ic

mag'ical

magi'cian

magiste'rial

mag'istrate

magnanim'ity

magnan'imous

mag'nate

magne'sia

mag'net

magnet'ic

mag'netism

mag'netize

magnet'o

magnif'icence

magnif'icent

magnif'icently

mag'nified

mag'nify

mag'nitude

mahog'any

maid

maid'en

mail

mail'able

mailed

maim

maimed

main

main'land

main'ly

main'spring

main'stay

maintain'

maintain'ed

main'tenance

maize

majes'tic

maj'esty

ma'jor

major'ity

make

ma'ker

make'shift

make'-up

mak'ing

maladjust'ment

mal'ady

mal'aise

mal'aprop

mala'ria

mal'content

male

malev'olent

mal'ice

mali'cious

mali'ciously

malign'

malig'nant		man'ly	
maligned'		mann'equin	
malin'ger		man'ner	
malin'gerer		man'nerly	
mal'leable		manoeu'vre	
mal'nutri'tion		manoeu'vring	
malt		man'-of-war'	
maltreat'		man'or	
maltreat'ed		man'power	
mama',		man'sion	
mamma'		man'slaughter	
mam'mal		man'tel	
mam'moth		man'telpiece	
man		mantil'la	
man'acle		man'tle	
man'age		man'ual	
man'agement		*manufac'-*	
man'ager		*ture*	
man'ageress		*manufac'-*	
manage'rial		*tured*	
man'date, *n.*		*manufac'turer*	
mandate', *v.*		*manufac'turing*	
man'datory		manure'	
man'dolin		man'uscript	
mane		man'y	
man'ful		map	
man'fully		ma'ple	
man'gle		mapped	
man'hood		mar	
ma'nia		mar'ble	
ma'niac		march (March)	
mani'acal		marched	
man'icure		march'ing	
man'ifest		mare	
manifesta'tion		mar'gin	
man'ifested		mar'ginal	
man'ifesting		marine'	
man'ifestly		mar'iner	
manifes'to		mar'ital	
man'ifold		mar'itime	
man'ikin		mark	
manip'ulate		marked	
manip'ulated		mar'ket	
manipula'tion		mar'malade	
mankind'		ma'rocain	
man'lier		marred	
		mar'riage	

mar'ried	
mar'ring	
mar'row	
mar'ry	
mar'rying	
marsh	
mar'shal	
mar'shalled,	
mar'shaled	
mart	
mar'tial	
mar'tyr	
mar'tyrdom	
mar'vel	
mar'velled,	
mar'veled	
mar'vellous,	
mar'velous	
marx'ist	
mascar'a	
mas'cot	
mas'culine	
mash	
mashed	
mask	
mas'ochism	
mas'ochist	
ma'son	
mason'ic	
ma'sonry	
masquerade'	
Mass, mass	
mas'sacre	
mas'sacred	
massage'	
masseur'	
masseuse'	
mass'ive	
mass'ively	
mast	
mas'ter	
mas'tered	
mas'terful	
mas'tering	
mas'terly	
mas'terpiece	
mas'tery	
mas'ticate	

mas'ticated	
mastica'tion	
mas'turbate	
masturba'tion	
mat	
match	
match'ing	
match'less	
mate	
mate'rial	
mate'rialist	
materialis'tic	
mate'rialize	
mater'nal	
mater'nity	
mathemat'ic	
mathemat'-	
ical	
mathemat'-	
ically	
mathemati'cian	
mathemat'ics	
mat'inée	
matric'ulate	
matric'ulated	
matricula'tion	
matrimo'nial	
mat'rimony	
ma'trix	
ma'tron	
ma'tronly	
mat'ter	
mat'ting	
mat'tress	
mature'	
matured'	
matu'rity	
maul	
mauled	
mausole'um	
mauve	
max'im	
max'imize	
max'imum	
may (May)	
may'be	
mayonnaise'	
may'or	

may'oral	
may'oralty	
may'oress	
maze	
me	
mead'ow	
mea'gre	
meal	
meal'time	
mean	
mean'est	
mean'ingless	
meant	
mean'time	
mean'while	
mea'sles	
meas'urable	
meas'ure	
meas'ured	
meas'urement	
meat	
mechan'ic	
mechan'ical	
mechan'- ically	
mech'anism	
mechaniza'tion	
mech'anize	
med'al	
med'dle	
med'dled	
med'dlesome	
me'dial	
me'diate	
media'tion	
me'diator	
med'ical	
medic'inal	
med'icine	
medie'val	
me'diocre	
medioc'rity	
med'itate	
med'itated	
medita'tion	
med'itative	
Mediterra'nean	
me'dium	

med'ley	
meek	
meek'ly	
meet	
meet'ing	
megaloman'ia	
meg'aphone	
meg'aton	
mel'ancholy	
mel'low	
mel'lowed	
melo'dious	
melodra'ma	
mel'ody	
mel'on	
melt	
melt'ed	
melt'ing	
mem'ber	
mem'bership	
mem'brane	
memen'to	
mem'oir	
mem'orable	
memoran'da	
memoran'dum	
memo'rial	
mem'orize	
mem'orized	
mem'orizing	
mem'ory	
men	
men'ace	
men'aced	
men'acing	
menag'erie	
mend	
menda'cious	
mend'ed	
men'dicant	
mend'ing	
me'nial	
men'opause	
men'tal	
mental'ity	
men'tion	
men'tioned	

men'tioning

men'u

mer'cantile

mer'cenary

mer'chandise

mer'chant

mer'ciful

mer'cifully

mer'ciless

mer'cury

mer'cy

mere

mere'ly

merge

mer'ger

merid'ian

meri'no

mer'it

merito'rious

mer'riment

mer'ry

mesh

meshed

mes'merize

mes'merized

mess

mes'sage

mes'senger

met

metab'olism

met'al

metal'lic

metall'urgy

met'aphor

metaphor'ical

metapsych'ics

mete

me'teor

meteor'ic

me'ter

meth'ane

meth'od

method'ical

Meth'odist

metic'ulous

me'tre

met'ric

met'rical

metrop'olis

metropol'itan

met'tle

Mex'ican

mias'ma

mi'ca

mice

Mich'aelmas

mi'crobe

microb'iol'ogy

mic'rofilm

mi'crophone

mi'croscope

microscop'ic

mi'crowave

mid

mid'day

mid'dle

mid'dle-aged

mid'dle-class

mid'dleman

midg'et

mid'night

midst

mid'summer

mid'way

mid'winter

mien

might

might'y

mi'grant

mi'grate

mi'grated

mil'age

mild

mild'er

mild'est

mild'dew

mild'ly

mild'ness

mile

mile'age

mile'stone

mil'ieu

mil'itant

mil'itarism

militaris'tic	mirac'ulous
mil'itary	mirage'
mil'itate	mire
mil'itated	mir'ror
mili'tia	mirth
milk	mirth'ful
mill	mi'ry
millen'nium	misapplied'
mill'er	misapply'
mill'ibar	misapprehend'
mill'iner	misapprehen'-
mill'inery	sion
mil'lion	misappropria'-
millionaire'	tion
mill'stone	misbehave'
mim'ic	misbeha'viour
mince	
mind	miscal'culate
mind'ed	miscal'culated
mind'ful	miscalcula'tion
mine	miscar'ry
mi'ner	miscella'neous
min'eral	miscel'lany
min'gle	mischance'
min'iature	mis'chief
min'imal	mis'chievous
min'imize	misconcep'tion
min'imum	(miscon'duct, *n.*
mi'ning	(misconduct', *v.*
min'ion	misconstruc'-
min'ister	tion
min'istered	miscon'strue
ministe'rial	misdeed'
min'istering	misdemean'-
ministra'tion	our
min'istry	misdirect'
mi'nor	mi'ser
minor'ity	mis'erable
min'ster	mis'ery
min'strel	misfit'
mint	misfor'tune
mint'ed	misgiv'ing
mi'nus	misguide'
minus'cule	misguid'ed
min'ute, *n., v.*	mishap'
minute', *adj.*	misinform'
minu'tiae	misinformed'
mir'acle	misinter'pret

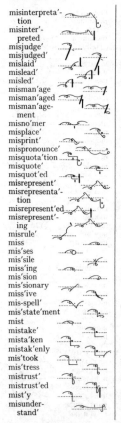

misinterpreta'-
tion
misinter'-
preted
misjudge'
misjudged'
mislaid'
mislead'
misled'
misman'age
misman'aged
misman'age-
ment
misno'mer
misplace'
misprint'
mispronounce'
misquota'tion
misquote'
misquot'ed
misrepresent'
misrepresenta'-
tion
misrepresent'ed
misrepresent'-
ing
misrule'
miss
mis'ses
mis'sile
miss'ing
mis'sion
mis'sionary
miss'ive
mis-spell'
mis'state'ment
mist
mistake'
mista'ken
mistak'enly
mis'took
mis'tress
mistrust'
mistrust'ed
mist'y
misunder-
stand'

misunder-
stand'ing
misunder'stood
misuse', v.
misuse', n.
mite
mit'igate
mit'igated
mitiga'tion
mix
mixed
mix'er
mix'ture
mnemon'ic
moan
mob
mobbed
mo'bile
mobil'ity
mobiliza'tion
mo'bilize
mock
mock'ery
mode
mod'el
mod'elled,
mod'eled
mod'erate,
n., a.
moderate', v.
mod'erately
modera'tion
mod'erator
mod'ern
mod'ernist
modernis'tic
moderniza'-
tion
mod'ernize
mod'est
mod'estly
mod'esty
mod'icum
modifica'tion
Moham'-
medan
Mo'hawk
Mohi'can

moi'ety	mon'ument
moist	monumen'- tal
mois'ten	
mois'tened	monumen'- tally
mois'ture	
mo'lar	mood
molas'ses	mood'ily
mold	mood'y
mol'ecule	moon
mole'hill	moon'light
molest'	moon'shine
molesta'tion	moor
molest'ed	moored
molest'ing	moor'land
mol'lify	mop
mol'ten	mope
mo'ment	mo'ped
mo'mentarily	mor'al
mo'mentary	morale'
momen'tous	mor'alist
momen'tum	moral'ity
mon'arch	mor'alize
monar'- chical	mor'alizing
	mor'ally
mon'archist	morass'
mon'astery	morato'rium
Mon'day	mor'bid
mon'etary	morbid'ity
mon'etize	*more*
mon'ey	*more*o'ver
mon'key	mor'ibund
	morn
mon'ogram	morn'ing
mon'ologue	moroc'co
mon'oplane	morose'
monop'olist	morose'ly
monop'olize	mor'phia
monop'oly	mor'row
monot'onous	mor'sel
monot'ony	mor'tal
monox'ide	mortal'ity
monsoon'	mor'tar
mon'ster	mort'gage
monstros'ity	mort'gaged
mon'strous	mortgagee'
mon'tage	mort'gager
month	mort'gaging
month'ly	mort'gagor

mortifica′tion	mourn′fully
mor′tified	mourn′ing
mor′tify	mouse
mor′tuary	mouse′-ear
mosa′ic	mouse′hole
mosqui′to	moustache′
moss	mouth
moss′y	mouth′ful
most	mouth′piece
most′ly	mov′able,
mote	move′able
motel	move
moth	moved
moth′er	move′ment
mo′ther-craft	mov′er
moth′erhood	mow (to
	grimace)
moth′er-*in*-law	(mow (to cut)
	(mow (of hay)
mo′tion	mowed
mo′tioned	mow′er
mo′tionless	Mr.
mot′ivate	*Mrs.*
motiva′tion	much
mo′tive	mud
mot′ley	mud′dle
mo′tor	mud′dled
mo′tor-bus	mud′dy
mo′tor-car	muf′fle
mo′tor-cy′cle	muf′fled
mo′torist	muf′ti
mot′orway	mug
mot′tled	mulat′to
mot′to	mul′berry
mould	mulct
mould′ed	mulct′ed
mould′er	mule
mould′ing	multifa′rious
mould′y	mul′tiple
mound	multiplica′tion
mount	multiplic′ity
moun′tain	mult′iplied
mountaineer′	mul′tiply
moun′tainous	mul′titude
mount′ebank	multitu′dinous
	mum′ble
mourn	mumps
mourn′er	munch
mourn′ful	

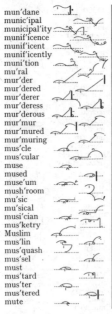

mun'dane	mu'tilate
munic'ipal	mu'tilated
municipal'ity	mutila'tion
munif'icence	mu'tiny
munif'icent	mut'ter
munif'icently	mut'tered
muni'tion	mut'tering
mu'ral	mut'ton
mur'der	mu'tual
mur'dered	muz'zle
mur'derer	muz'zled
mur'deress	my
mur'derous	myr'iad
mur'mur	myrrh
mur'mured	myr'tle
mur'muring	myself'
mus'cle	myste'rious
mus'cular	myste'riously
muse	mys'tery
mused	mys'tic
muse'um	mys'tical
mush'room	mys'tically
mu'sic	mys'ticism
mu'sical	mystifica'tion
musi'cian	mys'tified
mus'ketry	mys'tify
Muslim	mys'tifying
mus'lin	mystique'
mus'quash	myth
mus'sel	myth'ical
must	myth'ically
mus'tard	mytholog'ic
mus'ter	mytholog'ical
mus'tered	mytholog'ically
mute	mythol'ogy

N

nag
nail
nailed
nail'ing
naïve', naive'
na'ked
name
named
name'less
name'ly
nap
naph'tha
nap'kin
narcot'ic
narrate'
narra'ted
narra'tion
nar'rative
narra'tor
nar'row
nar'rowed
nar'rower
nar'rowest
nar'rowing
nar'rowly
nar'row-
    minded
na'sal
nas'ty
na'tal
na'tion
na'tional
na'tionalist
national'ity
nationaliza'-
    tion
na'tionalize
na'tionally
na'tive
nativ'ity

nat'ural
nat'uralist
naturaliza'tion
nat'uralize
nat'uralized
nat'urally
na'ture
na'turism
naught
naugh'ty
nau'sea
nau'seate
nau'tical
na'val
nave
nav'igable
nav'igate
nav'igated
naviga'tion
nav'igator
nav'vy
na'vy
nay
near
neared
near'er
near'est
near'ing
near'ly
neat
neat'er
neat'est
neat'ly
neb'ulous
nec'essarily
nec'essary
neces'sitate
neces'sitated
neces'sitating
neces'sitous

129

neces'sity		nes'tle	
neck		nes'tled	
neck'lace		net	
neck'tie		net'ted	
neck'wear		net'ting	
nec'tar		net'tle	
need		net'tled	
need'ed		net'work	
need'ful		neural'gia	
nee'dle		neurasthe'nia	
need'less		neurasthen'ic	
need'lessly		neuri'tis	
need'lessness		neurot'ic	
nee'dlework		neu'ter	
nefa'rious		neu'tral	
nega'tion		neutral'ity	
neg'ative		neu'tralize	
neglect'		neut'ron	
neglect'ed		nev'er	
neglect'ful		nev'ermore	
neglect'ing		*nevertheless'*	
négligé'		new	
neg'ligence		new'comer	
neg'ligent		new'er	
neg'ligently		new'est	
neg'ligible		newfan'gled	
negotiabil'ity		new-fash'ioned	
nego'tiable		new'ly	
nego'tiate		news	
nego'tiated		news'agent	
negotia'tion		news'paper	
ne'gress		news'print	
ne'gro		next	
ne'groid		nib	
neigh		nib'ble	
neigh'bour,		nib'bled	
neigh'bor		nib'bling	
neigh'bour-		nice	
hood		nice'ly	
nei'ther		ni'cest	
Nem'esis		ni'cety	
ne'on		niche	
neph'ew		nick	
Nep'tune		nick'el	
nerve		nick'name	
nerv'ous		nic'otine	
nerv'ously		niece	
nest		nig'gardly	

nigh
night
night'gown
night'ingale
night'ly
night'mare
night'shirt
night'wear
nil
nim'ble
nine
nineteen'
nineteenth'
nine'tieth
nine'ty
ninth
nip
nip'ple
ni'trate
ni'tric
ni'trogen
nitrog'enous
nit'wit
no
nobil'ity
no'ble
no'body
noctur'nal
nod
nod'ded
nod'ding
nog'gin
noise
noise'less
noise'lessly
nois'ily
nois'y
nom'ad
nomad'ic
no'menclature

nom'inal
nom'inate
nomina'tion
nominee'
non-accep'-
  tance

non-appear'-
  ance
non-arri'val
non-attend'-
  ance
non'chalance
non'chalant
non-com'-
  batant
non-commis'-
  sioned
non-commit'-
  tal
non-deliv'ery
non'descript
none
nonen'tity
non-interven'-
  tion
non-par'ty
nonpay'ment
non'plussed
non-res'ident
non'sense
nonsen'sical
non'-stop
nook
noon
noon'day
nor
nor'mal
Nor'man
north
north-east'
north-east'er
north-east'ern
north'erly
north'ern
north'erner
north'ward
north-west'
north-west'er
north-west'-
  erly
north-west'ern
Norwe'gian

nose		no'wise	
nos'tril		nox'ious	
not		noz'zle	
notabil'ity		nucleon'ics	
no'table		nu'cleus	
no'tary		nude	
nota'tion		nudge	
notch		nu'dism	
note		nu'dist	
note'book		nug'get	
note'worthy		nui'sance	
noth'ing		null	
no'tice		nul'lified	
no'ticeable		nul'lify	
no'ticed		nul'lity	
no'ticing		numb	
not'ifiable		numbed	
notifica'tion		num'ber	
no'tified		num'bered	
no'tify		num'bering	
no'tion		nu'meral	
notori'ety		numer'ical	
noto'rious		nu'merous	
notwithstand'-		nun	
ing		nup'tials	
nought		nurse	
noun		nursed	
nour'ish		nurs'ery	
nour'ished		nur'ture	
nour'ishment		nur'tured	
nov'el		nut	
nov'elist		nu'triment	
nov'elty		nutri'tion	
Novem'ber		nutri'tional	
nov'ice		nutri'tious	
now		nut'shell	
now'adays		nyl'on	
no'where		nymph	

O

O (oh)
oak
oar
oa'sis
oath
oat'meal
oats
ob'duracy
ob'durate
ob'durately
obe'dience
obe'dient
obe'diently
obese'
obes'ity
obey'
obey'ing
obit'uary
{ob'ject, n.
{object', v.
object'ed
object'ing
objec'tion
objec'tionable
objec'tive
objec'tively
obliga'tion

ob'ligatory
oblige'
obliged'
oblique'
oblit'erate
oblit'erated
oblitera'tion
obliv'ion
obliv'ious
ob'long
obnox'ious
obscure'

obscured'
obscu'rity
obse'quious

observ'ance
observ'ant
observa'tion
observe'
observed'
observ'er
observ'ing
obsess'
obsessed'
obses'sion
obsoles'cence
ob'solete
ob'stacle
ob'stinacy
ob'stinate
obstrep'erous
obstruct'
obstruct'ed
obstruct'ing
obstruc'tion
obstruc'tive
obtain'
obtain'able
obtained'
obtain'ing
obtrude'
obtru'ded
obtru'ding
obtru'sion
obtru'sive
obtru'sively
obtuse'
ob'viate
ob'viated
ob'viating
ob'vious

133

ob'viously		
occa'sion		
occa'sional		
occa'sioned		
occa'sioning		
oc'cident		
occiden'tal		
oc'cupancy		
oc'cupant		
occupa'tion		
oc'cupied		
oc'cupier		
oc'cupy		
oc'cupying		
occur'		
occurred'		
occur'rence		
occur'ring		
o'cean		
o'clock'		
oc'tagon		
octag'onal		
oc'tane		
oc'tave		
Octo'ber		
oc'ulist		
odd		
o'dious		
o'dium		
o'dorous		
o'dour, o'dor		
oes'trogen		
oes'trum		
of		
off		
offence'		
offend'		
offend'ed		
offend'er		
offend'ing		
offen'sive		
of'fer		
off'hand		
of'fice		
of'ficer		
offi'cial		
offi'cially		
offi'ciate		

offi'ciated		
offi'cious		
offi'ciously		
off'set, *n.*		
offset', *v.*		
off'spring		
oft'en		
oft'entimes		
oh		
oil		
oil'cloth		
oiled		
oil'skin		
oil'y		
oint'ment		
old		
old'er		
old'est		
old-fash'ioned		
ol'ive		
om'elet, om'elette		
o'men		
om'inous		
om'inously		
omis'sion		
omit'		
omit'ted		
omit'ting		
om'nibus		
omnip'otence		
omnip'otent		
omnis'cience		
omnis'cient		
omniv'orous		
on		
once		
on'cost		
one		
on'erous		
oneself'		
one'sided		
one'-way		
on'ion		
on'looker		
on'ly		
on'set		
on'slaught		

o'nus		o'ral	
on'ward		or'ange	
on'yx		ora'tion	
ooze		or'ator	
o'pal		or'atory	
opaque'		orb	
o'pen		or'bit	
open-air'		or'chard	
o'pened		or'chestra	
o'pener		orches'tral	
o'pening		or'chestrate	
o'penly		or'chid	
op'era		ordain'	
op'erate		ordained'	
operat'ic		or'deal	
opera'tion		or'der	
opera'tional		or'dered	
op'erative		or'dering	
op'erator		or'derliness	
operet'ta		or'derly	
opin'ion		or'dinal	
o'pium		or'dinance	
oppo'nent		or'dinarily	
opportune'		or'dinary	
opportu'nity		ord'nance	
oppose'		ore	
op'posite		or'gan	
opposi'tion		organ'ic	
oppress'		organ'ically	
oppressed'		or'ganism	
oppres'sion		or'ganist	
oppress'ive		organiza'tion	
oppress'ively		or'ganize	
oppress'or		or'ganizer	
op'tic		or'ganizing	
op'tical		or'gy	
opti'cian		o'rient	
op'timism		orien'tal	
op'timist		or'igin	
optimis'tic		orig'inal	
op'timum		original'ity	
op'tion		orig'inate	
op'tional		orig'inated	
op'ulence		orig'inating	
op'ulent		origina'tion	
op'us		orig'inator	
or			
or'acle			

or'nament	outnum'ber
ornamen'tal	outnum'bering
ornamenta'- tion	out-*of*-date'
	out-*of*-doors'
ornate'	out'put
or'phan	out'rage
or'thodox	outra'geous
os'cillate	out'right
oscilla'tion	out'set
os'cillograph	out'side
os'citancy	outsi'der
osten'sibly	out'size
ostenta'tion	out'skirts
ostenta'tious	outstand'ing
os'teopath	outstretch'
os'tracize	outstrip'
os'trich	outvote'
oth'er	out'ward
oth'erwise	out'wardly
ought	out'wards
ounce	outwit'
our	o'val
ours	ova'tion
ourselves'	ov'en
oust	o'ver
oust'ed	o'veralls
oust'ing	overbal'ance
out	overbal'anced
out'board	
out'break	overbear'ing
out'burst	o'verboard
out'cast	overbur'dened
out'come	overcame'
out'cry	o'vercast
out'dated'	(o'vercharge, *n.*
outdoors'	(overcharge', *v.*
out'er	o'vercoat
out'fit	overcome'
out'fitter	
out'going	overcom'ing
out'ing	over-con'fident
outland'ish	overcrowd'ed
out'law	over*do*'
out'lay	(o'verdose, *n.*
out'let	(overdose', *v.*
out'line	o'verdraft
out'look	overdrawn'
out'lying	overdue'

o'verflow, *n.*
overflow', *v.*
overgrown'
overhang'
overhaul'
overhauled'
overhead'
o'verheads
overhear'
overheard'
overjoyed'
o'verland
o'verload, *n.*
overload', *v.*
overlook'
o'verpass'
overpow'er
o'verride'

overruled'
o'verseas'
oversee'
o'verseer'
overshad'ow
o'vershoes
o'versight
o'verstaffed'
overstep'
overstrain'
overtake'
o'vertax, *n.*
overtax', *v.*

overthrow'
overthrown'
o'vertime
overtook'
o'verture
overturn'
o'verweight, *n.*
overweight', *v.*
overwhelm'
o'verwork, *n.*
overwork', *v.*
owe
owed
owes
ow'ing
owl
own
owned
own'er
own'ership
own'ing
ox
ox'en
ox'ide
oxidiza'tion
ox'idize
ox'ygen
oys'ter
oys'ter-shell
o'zone

P

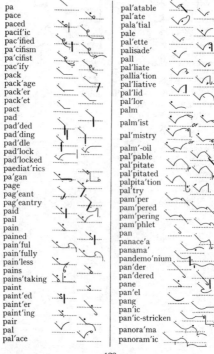

pa	pal'atable
pace	pal'ate
paced	pala'tial
pacif'ic	pale
pac'ified	pal'ette
pa'cifism	palisade'
pa'cifist	pall
pac'ify	pal'liate
pack	pallia'tion
pack'age	pal'liative
pack'er	pal'lid
pack'et	pal'lor
pact	palm
pad	
pad'ded	palm'ist
pad'ding	pal'mistry
pad'dle	
pad'lock	palm'-oil
pad'locked	pal'pable
paediat'rics	pal'pitate
pa'gan	pal'pitated
page	palpita'tion
pag'eant	pal'try
pag'eantry	pam'per
paid	pam'pered
pail	pam'pering
pain	pam'phlet
pained	pan
pain'ful	panace'a
pain'fully	panama'
pain'less	pandemo'nium
pains	pan'der
pains'taking	pan'dered
paint	pane
paint'ed	pan'el
paint'er	pang
paint'ing	pan'ic
pair	pan'ic-stricken
pal	
pal'ace	panora'ma
	panoram'ic

138

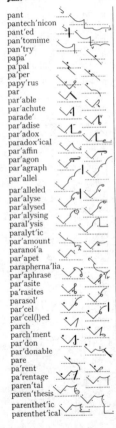

pant	par'ish
pantech'nicon	parish'ioner
pant'ed	Paris'ian
pan'tomime	par'ity
pan'try	park
papa'	par'king
pa'pal	par'lance
pa'per	par'ley
papy'rus	par'liament
par	parliamen'tary
par'able	
par'achute	par'lour
parade'	par'lous
par'adise	paro'chial
par'adox	par'ody
paradox'ical	parole'
par'affin	par'oxysm
par'agon	parquet', n., a.
par'agraph	par'quet, v.
par'allel	
par'alleled	par'rot
par'alyse	par'ry
par'alysed	pars'ec
par'alysing	parsimo'nious
paral'ysis	
paralyt'ic	par'simony
par'amount	pars'ley
paranoi'a	pars'nip
par'apet	par'son
parapherna'lia	part
par'aphrase	partake'
par'asite	part'ed
pa'rasites	par'tial
parasol'	partial'ity
par'cel	partic'ipant
par'cel(l)ed	partic'ipate
parch	partic'ipated
parch'ment	partic'ipating
par'don	participa'tion
par'donable	par'ticle
pare	*partic'ular*
pa'rent	partic'ularize
pa'rentage	*partic'ularly*
paren'tal	part'ing
paren'thesis	par'tisan
	parti'tion
parenthet'ic	parti'tioned
parenthet'ical	parti'tionist

part'ly	pa'tron
part'ner	pat'ronage
part'nership	pat'ronize
part'-time	pat'ter
par'ty	pat'tern
pass	pau'city
pass'able	pau'per
pas'sage	pause
passed	paused
pas'senger	paus'ing
pas'sion	pave
pas'sionate	pave'ment
pas'sive	pavil'ion
pas'sively	pav'ing
pass'port	paw
pass'word	pawn
past	pawn'broker
paste	pawned
paste'board	pawn'shop
pa'sted	pay
pas'tel	pay'able
pastiche'	payee'
pastille'	pay'er
pas'time	pay'ing
past'mas'ter	pay'master
pas'tor	pay'ment
pas'toral	pea
pa'stry	peace
pas'ture	peace'able
pat	peace'ful
patch	peace'fully
pat'ent	peach
pat'ented	peak
patentee'	peal
pater'nal	pealed
path	pear
pathet'ic	pearl
pathet'ically	peas'ant
pa'thos	peas'antry
pa'tience	peb'ble
pa'tient	peck
pa'tiently	pecula'tion
pa'triarch	pecu'liar
pat'riot	peculiar'ity
patriot'ic	pecu'liarly
pat'riotism	pecu'niary
patrol'	ped'agogic
patrolled'	ped'agogy

ped'al	
ped'ant	
pedan'tic	
ped'dle	
ped'estal	
pedes'trian	
ped'igree	
ped'lar	
peek	
peel	
peeled	
peel'ing	
peep	
peeped	
peep'ing	
peer	
peer'age	
peer'ing	
pee'vish	
pee'vishly	
peg	
pel'let	
pellu'cid	
pelt	
pelt'ed	
pen	
pe'nal	
pe'nalize	
pen'alty	
pen'ance	
pence	
pen'cil	
pen'cil(l)ed	
pend'ant	
pend'ent	
pend'ing	
pen'dulous	
pen'dulum	
pen'etrate	
pen'etrated	
penetra'tion	
penicill'in	
penin'sula	
pe'nis	
pen'itence	
pen'itent	
peniten'tiary	
pen'manship	

pen'niless	
pen'ny	
pen'sion	
pen'sioned	
pen'sioner	
pen'sioning	
pen'sive	
pent	
penu'rious	
pen'ury	
peo'ple	
peo'pled	
pep	
pep'per	
pep'sin	
per	
peram'bulate	
peram'bulator	
per an'num	
perceive'	
per cent'	
percent'age	
percep'tible	
percep'tion	
perch	
per'colate	
per'colator	
percus'sion	
perdi'tion	
per'emptory	
peren'nial	
per'fect	
per'fected	
perfec'tion	
per'fectly	
per'fidy	
per'forate	
perfora'tion	
perform'	
perform'ance	
performed'	
perform'er	
perform'ing	
{per'fume, *n*.	
{perfume', *v*.	
perfunc'tory	

perhaps'	
per'il	
per'ilous	
pe'riod	
period'ical	
per'iscope	
per'ish	
per'ishable	
per'ished	
per'jure	
per'jurer	
per'jury	
per'manency	
per'manent	
per'manently	
per'meate	
permis'sible	
permis'sion	
/per'mit, *n.*	
\permit', *v.*	
per'mutate	
perni'cious	
perox'ide	
perpendic'ular	
per'petrate	
per'petrated	
perpet'ual	
perpet'uate	
perpet'uated	
perpetu'ity	
perplex'	
perplex'ity	
per'quisite	
per'secute	
persecu'tion	
per'secutor	
persever'ance	
persevere'	
persevered'	
perseve'ringly	
Per'sian	
persist'	
persist'ence	
persist'ent	
persist'ently	
persist'ing	
per'son	

per'sonal	
personal'ity	
personifica'-	
tion	
personnel'	
perspec'tive	
perspicac'ity	
perspicu'ity	
perspira'tion	
perspire'	
persua'ded	
persua'sion	
persua'sive	
pert	
pertain'	
pertained'	
pertain'ing	
pertinac'ity	
per'tinent	
perturb'	
peru'sal	
peruse'	
pervade'	
perva'ded	
perverse'	
/per'vert, *n.*	
\pervert', *v.*	
pes'simism	
pes'simist	
pessimis'tic	
pest	
pes'ter	
pes'tered	
pes'tilence	
pes'tilent	
pet	
pet'al	
peti'tion	
peti'tioned	
peti'tioner	
pet'rified	
pet'rify	
pet'rol	
petro'leum	
pet'ted	
pet'ticoat	
pet'ty	

pet
pet'ulance	
pet'ulant	
pew	
pew'ter	
phan'tasy	
phan'tom	
pharmaceu'-tical	
phar'macist	
phar'macy	
phase	
phenobar'-bitone	
phenom'ena	
phenom'enal	
phenom'enon	
phi'al	
philanthrop'ic	
philan'thropist	
philan'thropy	
philat'elist	
philat'ely	
philharmon'ic	
philos'opher	
philosoph'ic	
philosoph'ical	
philos'ophy	
phlegmat'ic	
phob'ia	
phonet'ic	
phonet'ics	
phon'ograph	
phos'phate	
phos'phide	
phos'phorus	
pho'to	
pho'tograph	
photog'rapher	
photograph'ic	
photog'raphy	
photogravure'	
pho'ton	
phrase	
phys'ic	

phys'ical	
physi'cian	
phys'icist	
phys'ics	
physiog'raphy	
physiolog'ical	
physiol'ogy	
physiothe'rapist	
physiothe'rapy	
physique'	
pi'anist	
pian'o	
pianofor'te	
piaz'za	
pick	
pick'et	
pick'le	
pic'nic	
picto'rial	
pic'ture	
picturesque'	
pie	
piece	
piece'meal	
piece'-work	
pier	
pierce	
pierced	
pi'ety	
pig	
pig'eon	
pig'eonhole	
pig'iron	
pig'ment	
pig'my	
pile	
pil'fer	
pil'ferage	
pil'fered	
pil'ferer	
pil'fering	
pil'grim	
pil'grimage	
pill	
pil'lage	
pil'lar	
pil'lion	

pil'low		plac'id	
pi'lot		pla'giarism	
pin		pla'giarize	
pin'cers		plague	
pinch		plaid	
pine		plain	
pine'apple		plain'est	
pin'ion		plain'ly	
pin'ioned		plain'tiff	
pink		plain'tive	
pin'nacle		plait	
pint		plait'ed	
pin'-up		plan	
pioneer'		plane	
pi'ous		plan'et	
pi'ously		plank	
pip		planned	
pipe		plant	
pi'per		planta'tion	
pi'quancy		plant'ed	
pi'quant		plant'er	
pique		plas'ter	
pi'racy		plas'tered	
pi'rate		plas'terer	
pis'tol		plas'tic	
pis'ton		plate	
pit		plateau'	
pitch		plat'form	
pitch'er		plat'inum	
pit'eous		plat'itude	
pit'fall		platoon'	
pith		plausibil'ity	
pit'iable		plau'sible	
pit'iful		play	
pit'iless		played	
pit'ilessness		play'er	
pit'man		play'ful	
pit'-saw		play'fulness	
pit'tance		play'ground	
pit'y		play'ing	
piv'ot		play'mate	
piv'otal		play'room	
{plac'ard, *n*.		play'thing	
{placard', *v*.		plea	
placard'ed		plead	
placate'		pleas'ant	
place		pleas'antly	
placed		please	

pleas'urable	po'etry
pleas'ure	poign'ancy
pleat	poign'ant
plea'ted	point
plebe'ian	point'ed
pledge	point'er
ple'nary	point'ing
plen'teous	point'less
plen'tiful	poise
plen'ty	poi'son
pli'able	poi'sonous
pli'ant	poke
plied	po'lar
pli'ers	pole
plight	police'
plod	police'-court
plot	police'man
plough	pol'icy
ploughed	pol'io
plough'ing	pol'ish
pluck	pol'ished
plug	polite'
plum	pol'itic
plu'mage	polit'ical
plumb	politi'cian
plumb'er	pol'itics
plumb'ing	poll
plumb'-rule	pollute'
plume	pollu'tion
plumed	pol'tergeist
plump	polytech'nic
plun'der	pol'ythene
plun'dered	pomp
plunge	pom'pous
plu'ral	pond
plus	pon'der
plush	pon'dered
ply	pon'derous
pneumat'ic	pongee'
pneumo'nia	pontoon'
poach	po'ny
pock'et	pool
pock'et-book	pooled
po'em	pool'ing
po'et	poop
po'etess	poor
poet'ic	poor'er
poet'ical	poor'est

poor'house	possibil'ity	
pop	pos'sible	
pope	post	
pop'lar	post'age	
pop'lin	post'al	
pop'pycock	post'card	
pop'ulace	**post'code**	
pop'ular	post'date	
popular'ity	post dated	
popula'tion	post'er	
pop'ulous	poster'ity	
porce'lain	post'-free	
porch	post-haste'	
pore	post'humous	
pork	post'ing	
por'ous	post'man	
por'poise	post'mark	
por'ridge	post'master	
port	**post'paid**	
port'able	postpone'	
port'al	postponed'	
portend'	postpone'ment	
por'tent	postpon'ing	
porten'tous	post'script	
port'er	pos'ture	
portfo'lio	pot	
port'hole	pot'ash	
port'ico	potas'sium	
port'ière	pota'to	
por'tion	pota'toes	
port'ly	po'tency	
portman'teau	po'tent	
por'trait	poten'tial	
por'traiture	po'tion	
portray'	pot'ter	
portray'al	pot'tery	
portrayed'	pouch	
Portuguese'	poul'tice	
pose	poul'try	
poseur'	pounce	
posi'tion	pounced	
pos'itive	pounc'ing	
pos'itively	pound	
possess'	pour	
possessed'	poured	
posses'sion	pov'erty	
possess'ive	pow'der	
possess'or	pow'ders	

pow'er	
pow'erful	
pow'erless	
practicabil'ity	
prac'ticable	
prac'tical	
(prac'tice	
(prac'tise	
prac'tised	
prac'tising	
practi'tioner	
prai'rie	
praise	
praised	
praise'worthy	
prance	
pranced	
prank	
pray	
prayed	
prayer	
pray'ing	
preach	
preach'er	
preach'ing	
pream'ble	
preca'rious	
precau'tion	
precau'tionary	
precede'	
prece'dence	
prece'dent, *a.*	
prec'edent, *n.*	
pre'cept	
pre'cinct	
pre'cious	
prec'ipice	
precip'itate, *n., a.*	
precip'itate, *v.*	
precise'	
precise'ly	
precis'ion	
preclude'	
preco'cious	
precoc'ity	
preconceive'	

predeces'sor	
predic'ament	
predict'	
predict'able	
predict'ed	
predic'tion	
predispose'	
predom'inance	
predom'inant	
predom'inantly	
predom'inate	
pre-em'inence	
pre-em'inent	
pre'fab	
pref'ace	
pref'aced	
prefer'	
pref'erable	
pref'erence	
preferen'tial	
preferred'	
(pre'fix, *n.*	
(prefix', *v.*	
preg'nant	
prehistor'ic	
prej'udice	
prej'udiced	
prejudi'cial	
prejudi'cially	
prej'udicing	
prel'ate	
prelim'inary	
prel'ude	
premature'	
premed'itate	
premed'itated	
premedita'tion	
prem'ier	
prem'ise, *n.*	
premise', *v.*	
pre'mium	
pre-nat'al	
prepaid'	
prepara'tion	
prepar'atory	

prepare'		pretend'ed	
prepared'		pretend'ing	
prepar'ing		preten'tious	
prepon'der- ance		pre'text	
prepon'derat- ing		pret'ty	
		prevail'	
preposi'tion		prevailed'	
prepossess'ing		prevail'ing	
prepos'terous		prev'alence	
prereq'uisite		prev'alent	
		prevar'icate	
prerog'ative			
Presbyte'rian		prevar'icator	
pres'bytery			
prescribe'		prevent'	
prescribed'		prevent'ed	
prescri'ber		prevent'ing	
prescrip'tion		preven'tion	
pres'ence		pre'view	
pres'ent, n., a.		pre'vious	
present', v.		pre'viously	
present'able		prey	
presenta'tion		price	
pres'ently		priced	
preserva'tion		price'less	
preserv'ative		prick	
preserve'		prick'ly	
preserved'		pride	
preside'		priest	
pres'idency		pri'marily	
pres'ident		pri'mary	
presiden'tial		pri'mate	
presi'ding		prime	
press		pri'mer	
pressed		prime'val, primae'val	
press'ing		prim'itive	
pres'sure		prim'rose	
prestige'		prince	
presu'mably		prin'cess	
presume'		prin'cipal	
presumed'		prin'cipally	
presump'tion		prin'cipalship	
presump'tive		prin'ciple	
presump'tuous		print	
pretence'		print'ed	
pretend'		print'er	
		print'ing	

pri'or	
prior'ity	
pris'on	
pris'oner	
pri'vacy	
pri'vate	
priva'tion	
priv'ilege	
prize	
probabil'ity	
prob'able	
prob'ably	
pro'bate	
proba'tion	
proba'tionary	
probe	
probed	
prob'lem	
problemat'ic	
proce'dure	
proceed'	
pro'cess	
pro'cessed	
proces'sion	
proclaim'	
proclaimed'	
proclama'tion	
procliv'ity	
procon'sul	
procras'tinate	
procrastina'- tion	
proc'tor	
procur'able	
procure'	
prod	
prod'igal	
prodig'ious	
prod'igy	
prod'uce, n.	
produce', v.	
produ'cer	
prod'uct	
produc'tion	
produc'tive	
produc'tively	
productiv'ity	
profane'	

profan'ity	
profess'	
professed'	
profess'ing	
profes'sion	
profes'sional	
profes'sional- ism	
profes'sor	
prof'fer	
prof'fered	
profi'ciency	
profi'cient	
profi'ciently	
pro'file	
prof'it	
prof'itable	
prof'ited	
profiteer'	
prof'ligate	
profound'	
profuse'	
profu'sion	
prog'eny	
proges'terone	
prognos'tic	
prognostica'- tion	
pro'gramme, pro'gram	
pro'gress, n.	
progress', v.	
progres'sive	
prohib'it	
prohib'ited	
prohib'iting	
prohibi'tion	
prohibi'tive	
pro'ject, n.	
project', v.	
project'ed	
project'ing	
projec'tion	
project'or	
proleta'rian	
proleta'riat	
prolif'erate	

prolif'ic		propor'tionate	
pro'logue'		propor'tionately	
prolong'		propo'sal	
prolonga'tion		propose'	
prolonged'		proposed'	
promenade'		proposi'tion	
prom'inence		propound'	
prom'inent		propound'ed	
prom'inently		propri'etary	
promiscu'ity		propri'etor	
prom'ise		propri'ety	
prom'issory		propul'sion	
promote'		pro ra'ta	
promo'ted		prosa'ic	
promo'ter		prose	
promo'tion		pros'ecute	
prompt		pros'ecuted	
prompt'ed		prosecu'tion	
prompt'ing		pros'ecutor	
prompt'itude		pros'pect, n.	
prone		prospect', v.	
pro'noun		prospec'ted	
pronounce'		prospec'tive	
pronounce'-		prospec'tus	
ment		pros'per	
pronuncia'tion		pros'pered	
proof		prosper'ity	
prop		pros'perous	
propagan'da		pros'trate, a.	
prop'agate		prostrate', v.	
propaga'tion		prostra'ted	
propel'		prostra'tion	
propelled'		protect'	
propel'ler		protec'tion	
propen'sity		protec'tionist	
prop'er		protect'or	
prop'erly		pro'test, n.	
prop'erty		protest', v.	
proph'ecy, n.		Pro'testant	
proph'esied		protesta'tion	
proph'esy, v.		protest'ed	
proph'et		protest'ing	
prophet'ic		prot'on	
propi'tiate		protract'	
propi'tiated		protract'ed	
propi'tious		protrude'	
propor'tion		protrud'ed	
		proud	

proud'ly		publica'tion	
prove		public'ity	
proved		pub'licly	
prov'en		pub'lish	
prov'erb		pub'lished	
prover'bial		pub'lisher	
provide'		pub'lishing	
provi'ded		pud'ding	
prov'idence		pud'dle	
prov'ident		pu'erile	
prov'ince		puff	
provin'cial		pu'gilist	
provi'sion		pugna'cious	
provi'sional		pugnac'ity	
provi'so		puis'ne	
provoca'tion		pull	
provoc'ative		pulled	
provoke'		pulp	
provo'king		pul'pit	
prow'ess		pulsa'tion	
prowl		pulse	
prowled		pun'ice	
proxim'ity		pump	
prox'imo		pumped	
pru'dence		pump'ing	
pru'dent		punch	
pruden'tial		punch'-card	
pru'dently		punct'ual	
prune		punctual'ity	
Prus'sian		punct'uate	
pry		punct'uated	
psalm		punctua'tion	
pseu'do		punct'ure	
pseud'onym		pun'ish	
psychiat'ric		pun'ishment	
		pu'nitive	
psychi'atrist		pu'ny	
psychi'atry		pup	
psycho'an'alyst		pu'pil	
		pup'pet	
psycholog'ical		pur'chase	
psycholog'ically		pur'chaser	
psychol'ogist		pur'chase-tax	
psychol'ogy		pure	
psych'opath		pure'ly	
psychother'apist		purge	
pto'maine		purifica'tion	
pub'lic			
pub'lican			

pur′ified	
pur′ify	
pur′ity	
purloin′	
pur′ple	
pur′port, n.	
purport′, v.	
pur′pose	
pur′poseful	
pur′posely	
purse	
purs′er	
pursu′ant	
pursue′	
pursued′	
pursu′er	

pursuit′	
purvey′	
push	
pushed	
put	
pu′trefied	
pu′trefy	
pu′trid	
put′ter	
put′ting	
put′ty	
puz′zle	
puz′zled	
puz′zling	
pyjam′as	
pyl′on	
pyr′amid	

Q

quack
quacked
quad'rangle
quad'rant
quad'ruped
quad'ruple
quadru'plicate
quaff

quag'mire
quail
quaint
quake
quaked
qua'ker

qualifica'tion
qual'ified
qual'ify
qual'ity
qualm
quan'dary
quan'tify
quan'tity
qua'rantine
quar'rel
quar'reled,
    quar'relled
quar'relsome
quar'ry
quart
quar'ter
quar'terly
quar'termaster
quar'tern
quartet'
quar'to
quartz
quash
qua'ver
qua'vered

qua'vering
quay
quay'side
queen
queen'ly
queer
quell
quelled
quench
que'ried
quer'ulous
que'ry
quest
ques'tion
ques'tionable
ques'tionably
ques'tioned
ques'tioning
ques'tionnaire
queue
quib'ble
quick
quick'en
quick'ened
quick'er
quick'ly
quick'ness
quick'sand
quick'silver
quick'witted
quies'cent
qui'et
qui'eten
qui'etly
qui'etness
qui'etude
quie'tus
quill
quilt
quinine'

153

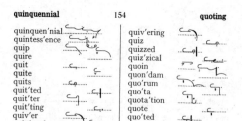

quinquen'nial	quiv'ering
quintess'ence	quiz
quip	quizzed
quire	quiz'zical
quit	quoin
quite	quon'dam
quits	quo'rum
quit'ted	quo'ta
quit'ter	quota'tion
quit'ting	quote
quiv'er	quo'ted
quiv'ered	quo'ting

R

rab'bi	raid	
rab'bit	rail	
rab'ble	rail'head	
rab'id	rail'ing	
race	rail'lery	
race'course	rail'road	
raced		
race'horse	rail'way	
ra'cer	rai'ment	
ra'cial	rain	
ra'cialism	rain'bow	
ra'cing	rain'drop	
ra'cist	rain'fall	
rack	rain'ing	
rack'et	rain'proof	
ra'dar	rain'-water	
ra'diance	rain'y	
ra'diant	raise	
ra'diate	raised	
ra'diated	rai'sin	
ra'diating	rake	
radia'tion	ral'lied	
ra'diator	ral'ly	
rad'ical	ral'lying	
ra'dii	ram	
ra'dio	ram'ble	
radioac'tive	ram'bler	
ra'diogram	ramifica'tion	
radiol'ogist	rammed	
rad'ishes	ramp	
rad'ium	rampage'	
ra'dius	ram'pant	
raf'fle	ram'part	
raf'fled	ram'shackle	
raft	ran	
raft'er	ranch	
rag	ran'cid	
rage	ran'cour,	
rag'ged	ran'cor,	
ra'ging	rand	

155

ran'dom		ra'tionalize	
rang		rat'tle	
range		rau'cous	
ran'ger		rav'age	
rank		rave	
ranked		rav'el	
ran'kle		ra'ven	
ran'kled		rav'enous	
ran'sack		ravine'	
ran'som		rav'ish	
rant		rav'ished	
rap		raw	
rapa'cious		ray	
rapac'ity		raze	
rap'id		ra'zor	
rapid'ity		reach	
rap'idly		reached	
ra'pier		reach'ing	
rapped		react'	
rap'ping		react'ed	
rapt		reac'tion	
rap'ture		reac'tionary	
rap'turous		reac'tor	
rare		read	
rare'ly		read, *p.t.*	
rar'ity		read'able	
ras'cal		readdress'	
rascal'ity		read'er	
rash		read'ier	
rash'ly		read'ily	
rasp		read'iness	
rasp'berry		read'ing	
rat		readjust'	
rat'able		readjust'ed	
ratch'et		readjust'ment	
rate		readmis'sion	
rate'able		readmit'	
rate'payers		read'y	
rath'er		read'ymade	
ratifica'tion		reaffirm'	
rat'ified		re'al	
rat'ify		re'alism	
ra'ting		re'alist	
ra'tio		realist'ic	
ra'tion		real'ity	
ra'tional		re'alizable	
rationaliza'-tion		realiza'tion	
		re'alize	

re'alized	recant'
re'alizing	recapit'ulate
re'ally	recapitula'tion
realm	recap'ture
ream	recast'
rean'imate	recede'
reap	rece'ded
reaped	rece'ding
reap'er	receipt'
reap'ing	receiv'able
reappear'	receive'
reappear'ance	received'
reappoint'	receiv'er
reappoint'ment	receiv'ership
reappor'tion	re'cent
rear	re'cently
reared	recep'tacle
re-arrange'	recep'tion
re-arrange'-	recep'tionist
ment	recep'tive
rea'son	receptiv'ity
rea'sonable	recess'
rea'sonably	reces'sion
rea'soned	reces'sional
reassem'ble	re'charge'
reassert'	rec'ipe
reassu'rance	recip'ient
reassure'	recip'rocal
re'bate, n.	recip'rocate
rebate', v.	reciproca'tion
reb'el, n.	reciproc'ity
rebel', v.	reci'tal
rebelled'	recita'tion
rebell'ion	recite'
rebell'ious	reci'ted
rebound'	reci'ting
rebuff'	reck'less
rebuild'	reck'lessness
rebuild'ing	reck'on
rebuilt'	reck'oned
rebuke'	reck'oning
rebut'	reclaim'
rebut'tal	reclaimed'
rebut'ting	reclama'tion
recal'citrant	recline'
recall'	reclined'
recalled'	recli'ning
recall'ing	recluse'

recogni'tion	rectan'gular
recog'nizance	rec'tify
recog'nizant	rec'tifying
rec'ognize	rec'titude
rec'ognized	rec'tor
recoil'	recum'bent
recoiled'	recu'perate
recollect'	recu'perated
recollec'tion	recu'perating
recommend'	recupera'tion
recommenda'-	recu'perative
tion	recur'
rec'ompense	recurred'
rec'oncile	recur'rence
rec'onciled	recur'rent
reconcilia'tion	recur'ring
recondi'tion	red
reconnoi'tre	redeem'
reconsid'er	redeem'able
reconsidera'-	redeemed'
tion	redemp'tion
reconsid'ered	redeploy'
reconsid'ering	red'-hot
reconstruct'	redistrib'ute
reconstruct'ed	red'olent
reconstruct'ing	redoub'le
reconstruc'tion	redound'
{rec'ord, n.	redound'ed
{record', v.	redraft'
record'er	redress'
recount'	reduce'
recount'ed	reduced'
recount'ing	redu'cing
recoup'	reduc'tion
recourse'	redun'dant
recov'er	re-ech'o
recov'erable	re-ech'oed
recov'ered	reed
recov'ery	reef
rec'reant	reef'er
rec'reate	reek
recrea'tion	reel
recrim'inate	re-elect'
recrimina'tion	re-elect'ed
recruit'	re'-elec'tion
recruit'ed	reeled
recruit'ment	re-embark'
rect'angle	re-enact'

re-enact'ment	refrig'erate
re-enforce'	refrig'erated
re-engage'	refrig'erating
re-en'ter	refrigera'tion
re-en'tered	refrig'erator
re-estab'lish	ref'uge
re-estab'lished	refugee'
re-estab'lishment	refund'
re'-examina'tion	refund'ed
re-exam'ine	refund'ing
refer'	refu'sal
referee'	⎰ref'use, n., a.
ref'erence	⎱ refuse', v.
referen'dum	refuta'tion
	refute'
referred'	refu'ted
refer'ring	refu'ting
refill'	regain'
refine'	regained'
refine'ment	re'gal
refi'ner	regale'
refi'nery	regaled'
refit'	rega'lia
reflect'	re'gally
reflect'ed	regard'
reflec'tion	regard'ed
reflec'tive	regard'ing
reflect'or	regard'less
re'flex, n., adj.	re'gency
reflex', v.	regen'erate, n., adj.
reform', v.	regen'erate, v.
reforma'tion	regen'erated
reform'atory	regenera'tion
reformed'	re'gent
reform'er	régime'
reform'ing	reg'imen
refrac'tion	reg'iment
	regimen'tal
refrac'tory	re'gion
refrain'	re'gional
refrained'	reg'ister
refresh'	reg'istered
refresh'ing	reg'istering
refresh'ment	reg'istrar
	registra'tion
	registrat'or
	reg'istry

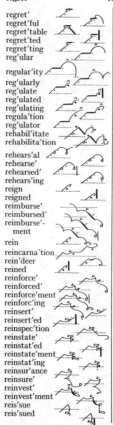

regret'	reit'erate
regret'ful	reit'erated
regret'table	reitera'tion
regret'ted	reject'
regret'ting	reject'ed
reg'ular	rejec'tion
	rejoice'
regular'ity	rejoiced'
reg'ularly	rejoin'
reg'ulate	rejoin'der
reg'ulated	rejoined'
reg'ulating	relapse'
regula'tion	
reg'ulator	relapsed'
rehabil'itate	relate'
rehabilita'tion	rela'ted
	rela'tion
rehears'al	rela'tionship
rehearse'	rel'ative
rehearsed'	rel'atively
rehears'ing	relativ'ity
reign	relax'
reigned	relax'ation
reimburse'	relaxed'
reimbursed'	relay', n.
reimburse'-	re-lay', v.
ment	release'
rein	released'
reincarna'tion	releas'ing
rein'deer	rel'egate
reined	relega'tion
reinforce'	relent'
reinforced'	relent'ed
reinforce'ment	relent'ing
reinforc'ing	relent'less
reinsert'	rel'evancy
reinsert'ed	rel'evant
reinspec'tion	
reinstate'	reliabil'ity
reinstat'ed	reli'able
reinstate'ment	reli'ance
reinstat'ing	reli'ant
reinsur'ance	rel'ic
reinsure'	relied'
reinvest'	relief'
reinvest'ment	relieve'
reis'sue	relieved'
reis'sued	reliev'ing
	relig'ion

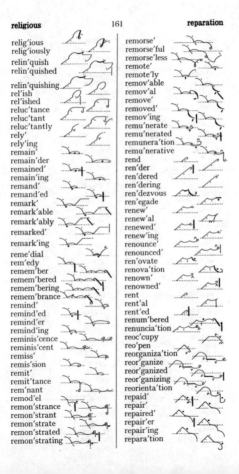

relig′ious	remorse′
relig′iously	remorse′ful
relin′quish	remorse′less
relin′quished	remote′
relin′quishing	remote′ly
rel′ish	remov′able
rel′ished	remov′al
reluc′tance	remove′
reluc′tant	removed′
reluc′tantly	remov′ing
rely′	remu′nerate
rely′ing	remu′nerated
remain′	remunera′tion
remain′der	remu′nerative
remained′	rend
remain′ing	ren′der
remand′	ren′dered
remand′ed	ren′dering
remark′	ren′dezvous
remark′able	ren′egade
remark′ably	renew′
remarked′	renew′al
remark′ing	renewed′
reme′dial	renew′ing
rem′edy	renounce′
remem′ber	renounced′
remem′bered	ren′ovate
remem′bering	renova′tion
remem′brance	renown′
remind′	renowned′
remind′ed	rent
remind′er	rent′al
remind′ing	rent′ed
reminis′cence	renum′bered
reminis′cent	renuncia′tion
remiss′	reoc′cupy
remis′sion	reo′pen
remit′	reorganiza′tion
remit′tance	reor′ganize
rem′nant	reor′ganized
remod′el	reor′ganizing
remon′strance	reorienta′tion
remon′strant	repaid′
remon′strate	repair′
remon′strated	repaired′
remon′strating	repair′er
	repair′ing
	repara′tion

repartee'	
repass'	
repast'	
repay'	
repay'able	
repay'ment	
repeal'	
repealed'	
repeat'	
repeat'edly	
repeat'ing	
repel'	
repelled'	
repel'lent	
repent'	
repent'ance	
repent'ant	
repent'ed	
repent'ing	
repercus'sion	
repertoire'	
rep'ertory	
repeti'tion	
repeti'tious	
repet'itive	
repine'	
repined'	
repi'ning	
replace'	
replace'able	
replace'ment	
replen'ish	
replen'ished	
replen'ishing	
replete'	
reple'tion	
rep'lica	
replied'	
reply'	
reply'ing	
report'	
report'ed	
report'er	
report'ing	
repose'	
repos'itory	
reprehend'	
reprehensible	

reprehen'sion	
represent'	
representa'tion	
represent'ative	
represent'ed	
represent'ing	
repress'	
repressed'	
repres'sion	
reprieve'	
reprieved'	
repriev'ing	
(rep'rimand, *n.*	
(reprimand', *v.*	
(re'print, *n.*	
(reprint', *v.*	
reprint'ed	
repri'sal	
reproach'	
reproached'	
reproach'ful	
reproach'fully	
reproach'ing	
rep'robate	
reproduce'	
reproduc'tion	
reproduc'tive	
reproof'	
reprove'	
reproved'	
rep'tile	
repub'lic	
repub'lican	
republica'tion	
repub'lish	
repub'lished	
repu'diate	
repu'diated	
repu'diating	
repudia'tion	
repug'nance	
repug'nant	
repulse'	
repulsed'	
repuls'ing	
repul'sion	

repul'sive	res'idency
repul'sively	res'ident
rep'utable	residen'tial
reputa'tion	resid'ual
repute'	resid'uary
repu'ted	res'idue
request'	resign'
request'ed	resigna'tion
request'ing	resigned'
req'uiem	resign'ing
require'	resil'ience
required'	resil'iency
require'ment	resil'ient
requir'ing	res'in
req'uisite	resist'
requisi'tion	resist'ance
requisi'tioned	resist'ed
requisi'tioning	res'olute
requi'tal	res'olutely
requite'	resolu'tion
requi'ted	resolve'
re-read'	resolved'
re-read', *p.t.*	resolv'ing
rescind'	res'onance
rescind'ed	res'onant
res'cue	resort'
res'cued	resort'ed
res'cuer	resound'
res'cuing	resound'ed
research'	resource'
resem'blance	resource'ful
resem'ble	respect'
resem'bled	respect'ability
resent'	respect'able
resent'ed	
resent'ful	respect'ably
resent'ing	respect'ed
resent'ment	respect'ful
reserva'tion	respect'fully
reserve'	respect'ing
reserved'	respect'ive
reserv'ing	respect'ively
res'ervoir	respira'tion
reset'	
reship'ment	res'pirator
reside'	respir'atory
resi'ded	res'pite
res'idence	resplen'dent

respond'		resuscita'tion	
respond'ed		re'tail, n., a.	
respon'der		retail', v.	
respond'ing		retail'er	
response'		retain'	
responsibil'- ities		retained'	
{responsibil'- ity		retal'iate	
respon'sible		retal'iated	
respon'sive		retal'iating	
rest		retalia'tion	
res'taurant		retard'	
restau'rateur		retard'ed	
rest'ed		reten'tion	
rest'ful		reten'tive	
rest'fully		ret'icence	
rest'fulness		ret'icent	
rest'ing		ret'ina	
restitu'tion		ret'inue	
rest'ive		retire'	
rest'less		retired'	
rest'lessly		retire'ment	
rest'lessness		retir'ing	
restora'tion		retort'	
restor'ative		retort'ed	
restore'		retouch'	
restored'		retrace'	
restrain'		retraced'	
restrained'		retra'cing	
restrain'ing		retract'	
restraint'		retreat'	
restrict'		retreat'ed	
restrict'ed		retreat'ing	
restrict'ing		retrench'	
restric'tion		retrench'ment	
result'		retribu'tion	
result'ant		retrieve'	
result'ed		retrieved'	
resume'		retriev'er	
résumé'		retriev'ing	
resumed'		ret'rograde	
resu'ming		ret'rograded	
resump'tion		ret'rospect	
resump'tive		retrospec'tion	
resurge'		retrospec'tive	
resurrec'tion		retrospec'tively	
resus'citate		return'	
		return'able	
		returned'	

return'ing		revolt'	
reu'nion		revolt'ed	
reunite'		revolt'ing	
revalua'tion		revolu'tion	
reveal'		revolu'tionary	
revealed'		revolu'tionize	
reveal'ing		revolve'	
rev'el		revolved'	
revela'tion		revolv'er	
rev'elry		revul'sion	
revenge'		reward'	
revenged'		reward'ed	
revenge'ful		reward'ing	
rev'enue		rewrite'	
		rewrit'ten	
rever'berate		rhap'sody	
rever'berated		rhe'ostat	
reverbera'tion		rhes'us	
reverb'erator		rhet'oric	
revere'		rhetor'ical	
revered'		rheumat'ic	
rev'erence		rheum'atism	
rev'erend		rhen'matoid	
rev'erent			
rev'erie		rhinoc'eros	
revers'al		rhu'barb	
reverse'		rhyme	
reversed'		rhythm	
revers'ible		rhyth'mic	
revert'		rhyth'mical	
revert'ed		rib	
revert'ing		rib'ald	
review'		rib'bon	
reviewed'		rice	
review'er		rich	
review'ing		rich'er	
revile'		rich'es	
revise'		rich'est	
revised'		rich'ly	
revi'sing		rid	
revi'sion		rid'dance	
revi'sionary		rid'dle	
revi'sionist		ride	
revis'it		ri'der	
revi'val		ridge	
revive'		rid'icule	
revived'		rid'iculed	
revoke'		ridic'ulous	

ridic′ulously		ri′pened	
rid′ing		ri′pening	
rife		ripped	
riff′raff		rip′ping	
ri′fle		rip′ple	
ri′fled		rise	
ri′fling		ris′en	
rift		risibil′ity	
rig		ris′ible	
right		ri′sing	
right′-angle		risk	
right′-angled		risked	
right′eous		risk′ing	
right′eousness		risk′y	
right′ful		ris′qué	
right′fulness		rite	
right′-hand		rit′ual	
right′ing		ri′val	
right′ly		ri′val(l)ed	
rig′id		ri′val(l)ing	
rigid′ity		ri′valry	
rig′or		riv′er	
rig′orous		riv′et	
rig′our		riv′eted	
rile		riv′eting	
riled		road	
ri′ling		road′hog	
rim		road′side	
rime		road′ster	
rind		road′way	
ring		road′worthy	
ringed		roam	
ring′er		roamed	
ring′ing		roam′er	
ring′leader		roan	
ring′let		roar	
ring′-road		roared	
rink		roast	
rinse		roast′ed	
rinsed		roast′er	
rins′ing		roast′ing	
ri′ot		rob	
ri′oter		rob′ber	
ri′otous		rob′bery	
ri′otously		robe	
rip		rob′in	
ripe		rob′ot	
ri′pen		robust′	

robust'ly	rotate'
rock	rota'ted
rock'er	rota'tion
rock'ery	rote
rock'et	rot'ted
rock'ing	rot'ten
rod	rot'ting
rode	rotund'
ro'dent	rotund'ity
rode'o	rou'ble
roe	rouge
rogue	rough
rogu'ish	rough'en
rogu'ishly	rough'er
rôle	rough'ly
roll	round
rolled	round'about
roll'er	round'ed
roll'ing	round'ing
roll'ing-stock	round'ly
ro'man,	rouse
Ro'man	roused
romance'	rous'ing
roman'tic	rout
romp	route
romped	routine'
romp'ing	rove
rood	ro'ver
roof	ro'ving
roof'ing	row (a rank)
roof'less	row (a tumult)
room	row'diness
room'y	row'dy
roost	row'dyism
roost'er	rowed
root	row'lock
root'ed	roy'al
rope	roy'alist
ro'sary	roy'ally
rose	roy'alty
ro'seate	rub
ros'in	rubbed
ros'ter	rub'ber
ros'trum	rub'bing
ro'sy	rub'bish
rot	ru'by
Rotar'ian	ruc'tion
ro'tary	rudder

rude		run	
rude'ness		run'away	
ru'diment		run'-down'	
rudimen'tal		run'way	
rudimen'tary		rung	
rue		run'ner	
rued		run'ning	
rue'ful		rupee'	
rue'fully		rup'ture	
ruf'fian		rup'tured	
ruf'fle		ru'ral	
ruf'fled		ruse	
ruf'fling		rush	
rug		rushed	
rug'ged		rush'ing	
ru'in		rusk	
ruina'tion		rus'set	
ru'ined		Rus'sian	
ru'ining		rust	
ru'inous		rus'tic	
rule		rus'ticate	
ruled		rust'ing	
ru'ler		rus'tle	
ru'ling		rus'tled	
rum		rus'tling	
rumble		rust'y	
ru'minate		rut	
rum'mage		ruth	
ru'mour,		ruth'less	
ru'mor		ruth'lessly	
rump		ruth'lessness	
rum'ple		rye	
rum'pled		ry'ot	

S

Sab'bath
sa'ble
sabotage'
sa'bre
sack
sack'ing
sac'rament
sa'cred
sac'rifice
sac'rificed
sac'rilege
sacrile'gious
sad
sad'den
sad'der
sad'dest
sad'dle
sad'dled
sad'dler
sa'dism
sad'ly
safa'ri
safe
safe-con'duct
safe'-depos'it
safe'guard
saf'er
saf'est
safe'ty
saga'cious
sagac'ity
sage
said
sail
sailed
sail'ing
sail'or
saint
saint'ly
sake

sal'ad
sal'aried
sal'ary
sale
sale'able
sales'man
sales'manship
sales'woman
sa'lient
salin'ity
sal'low
sall'y
salm'on
saloon'
salt
salt'ed
salt'ing
salu'brious
sal'utary
saluta'tion
salute'
salu'ted
sal'vage
salva'tion
salve
salved
Samar'itan
same
sam'ple
sanato'rium
sanc'tified
sanc'tify
sanc'tion
sanc'tioned
sanc'tioning
sanc'tity
sanc'tuary
sanc'tum
sand
san'dal

sand'stone	saun'tered
sand'wich	saun'tering
sand'y	sau'sage
sane	sav'age
sang	sav'agely
san'guine	save
san'itary	sa'viour
sanita'tion	sa'vour,
san'ity	sa'vor
sank	sa'voury
sap	savoy'
sap'per	saw
sap'phire	saw'dust
sar'casm	sawed
sarcas'tic	saw'ing
sarcas'tically	saw'mill
sardine'	sawn
sa'ri	saw'yer
sarong'	Sax'on
sarsaparil'la	sax'ophone
sartor'ially	say
sash	say'ing
sat	says
satch'el	scab'bard
sate	scaf'fold
sa'ted	scaf'folding
sateen'	scald
sa'tiate	scale
sa'tiated	scaled
sati'ety	scalp
sat'in	scamped
sat'ire	scam'per
satir'ical	scam'pered
sat'irist	scam'pering
satisfac'tion	scam'pi
satisfac'torily	scan
satisfac'tory	scan'dal
sat'isfied	scan'dalous
sat'isfy	scan'ner
sat'urate	scant
sat'urated	scant'ily
sat'urating	scant'ly
satura'tion	scant'y
Sat'urday	scar
sauce	scarce
sauce'pan	scarce'ly
sau'cer	scarce'ness
saun'ter	scar'city

scare	scientif'ic
scare'monger	scientif'ically
scarf	sci'entist
sca'ring	scin'tillating
scar'let	scis'sors
scarred	scoff
scathe	scoffed
sca'thing	scoff'er
scat'ter	scoff'ing
scat'tered	scold
scat'tering	scone
scenar'io	scoop
scene	scoot'er
sce'nery	scope
sce'nic	scorch
scent	score
scent'ed	scored
scep'tic,	scor'er
skep'tic	scor'ing
scep'tical	scorn
scep'ticism	scorn'ful
scep'tre	scorn'fully
sched'ule	scorn'ing
sched'ule (U.S.)	Scot
sched'uled	Scotch, scotch
scheme	Scots'man
sche'mer	Scot'tish
schizophren'ia	scoun'drel
schnör'kel	scour
	scourge
schol'ar	scout
schol'arly	scowl
schol'arship	scowled
scholas'tic	scowl'ing
school	scram'ble
school'boy	scram'bled
schooled	scram'bling
school'fellow	scrap
	scrape
school'girl	scratch
school'house	scrawl
school'master	scrawled
school'mistress	scream
school'room	screamed
school'teacher	screech
schoon'er	screen
sciat'ica	screened
sci'ence	screw

screwed	search'er
scrib'ble	search'ing
scrib'bled	search'light
scrim'mage	sea'shore
scrip	sea'side
script	sea'son
Scrip'ture	sea'sonable
scriv'ener	sea'sonal
scroll	sea'soned
scrounge	seat
scrub	seat'ed
scrubbed	seat'ing
scru'ple	sea'ward
scru'pulous	sea'weed
scru'pulously	sea'worthy
scru'pulous-	secede'
ness	seclude'
scru'tinize	seclu'sion
scru'tiny	seclu'sive
scuf'fle	Sec'onal
scuf'fled	sec'ond
scull	sec'ondary
scull'er	sec'onded
scull'ery	sec'onder
sculp'tor	sec'ond-hand
sculp'ture	sec'ondly
scum	sec'ond-rate
scur'ried	sec'onds
scur'rilous	se'crecy
scur'ry	se'cret
scut'tle	secreta'rial
scythe	secreta'riat
sea	sec'retary
sea'board	secrete'
sea'borne	secre'ted
sea'-coast	secre'tion
sea'faring	se'cretive
seal	sect
sealed	secta'rian
sea'-level	sec'tion
seal'skin	sec'tional
seam	sec'tionalize
sea'man	sec'tor
sea'manship	sec'ular
seamed	secure'
sea'plane	secured'
sea'port	secure'ly
search	secu'ring

secu'rity	
sedate'	
sed'entary	
sed'iment	
sedi'tion	
sedi'tious	
see	
seed	
see'ing	
seek	
seem	
seemed	
seem'ingly	
seen	
seethe	
seeth'ing	
seg'ment	
seg'regate	
segrega'tion	
segrega'tionist	
seismol'ogy	
seize	
seized	
seiz'ing	
sei'zure	
sel'dom	
select'	
select'ed	
select'ing	
selec'tion	
select'ive	
select'or	
self	
self-addressed'	
self'-assur'ance	
self-con'fidence	
self-con'scious	
self-contained'	
self-control'	
self-defence'	
self-determina'-tion	
self-esteem'	
self-ev'ident	
self-explan'-atory	
self-in'terest	

self'ish	
self'ishly	
self'ishness	
self-possessed'	
self-posses'sion	
self-reli'ance	
self-respect'	
self-service'	
self-willed'	
sell	
sell'er	
Sel'lotape	
selves'	
sem'aphore	
sem'blance	
sem'ibreve	
sem'icircle	
sem'icolon	
sem'inar	
sem'inary	
sen'ate	
sen'ator	
send	
send'er	
se'nile	
senil'ity	
se'nior	
senior'ity	
sensa'tion	
sensa'tional	
sense	
sense'less	
sense'lessly	
sense'lessness	
sensibil'ity	
sen'sible	
sen'sitive	
sen'sitively	
sen'sitiveness	
sen'sual	
sent	
sen'tence	
sen'tenced	
sen'tient	
sen'timent	
sentimen'tal	
sen'tinel	

sen'try		seventeenth'	
sep'arate, *adj.*		sev'enth	
sep'arate, *v.*		sev'entieth	
sep'arated		sev'enty	
sep'arating		sev'er	
separa'tion		*sev'eral*	
sep'arator		*sev'erally*	
Septem'ber		sev'erance	
sep'tic		severe'	
sepul'chral		sev'ered	
sep'ulchre		severe'ly	
se'quel		sev'ering	
se'quence		sever'ity	
seques'tered		sew	
serenade'		sew'age	
serene'		sewed	
serene'ly		sew'er	
seren'ity		sew'erage	
serge		sew'ing	
ser'geant		sewn	
se'rial		sex	
seria'tim		sex'ton	
se'ries		sex'y	
se'rious		shab'by	
se'riously		shack	
se'riousness		shack'le	
ser'jeant		shack'led	
ser'mon		shade	
serv'ant		shad'ow	
serve		shad'owy	
served		sha'dy	
serv'ice		shaft	
serv'iceable		shaft'ing	
serv'ile		shake	
servil'ity		sha'ken	
serv'ing		sha'ker	
serv'itude		sha'ky	
ses'sion		*shall*	
set		shal'low	
set'back		shal'lower	
set'ting		sham	
set'tle		shame	
set'tled		shamed	
set'tlement		shame'ful	
set'tler		shame'fully	
set'tling		shame'less	
sev'en		shampoo'	
seventeen		shampooed'	

shampoo'ing	
sham'rock	
shape	
shape'less	
share	
shared	
share'holder	
sha'ring	
shark	
sharp	
sharp'en	
shar'pened	
shar'pening	
sharp'er	
sharp'est	
sharp'ly	
shat'ter	
shat'tered	
shave	
shaved	
shav'ing	
shawl	
she	
sheaf	
shear	
sheared	
shear'ing	
shears	
sheath	
sheathe	
sheaves	
shed	
sheen	
sheep	
sheep'ish	
sheep'ishly	
sheer	
sheet	
sheet'ing	
shelf	
shell	
shellac'	
shellacked'	
shelled	
shell'fish	
shel'ter	
shel'tered	
shel'tering	

shelve	
shemoz'zle	
shep'herd	
sher'bet	
sher'iff	
sher'ry	
shield	
shield'ed	
shield'ing	
shift	
shift'ed	
shift'ing	
shift'less	
shift'y	
shil'ling	
shim'mer	
shim'mered	
shim'mering	
shin	
shine	
shin'gle	
shi'ning	
shi'ny	
ship'builder	
ship'building	
ship'ment	
ship'owner	
ship'per	
ship'ping	
ship'yard	
shire	
shirk	
shirked	
shirk'er	
shirk'ing	
shirt	
shiv'er	
shiv'ered	
shiv'ering	
shoal	
shock	
shod	
shod'dy	
shoe	
shoe'maker	
shone	

shook	shrine
shoot	shrink
shoot'ing	shrink'age
shop	shrink'ing
shop'keeper	shriv'el
shop'ping	shroud
shop'-stew'ard	shroud'ed
shore	shrub
shorn	shrug
short	shrunk
short'age	shrunk'en
short'bread	shud'der
short'-circ'uit	shud'dered
short'coming	shuf'fle
short'en	shuf'fled
short'er	shun
short'est	shunt
short'hand	shunt'ed
short'ly	shunt'ing
shorts	shut
short'sighted	shut'ter
short'-term	shut'tle
shot	shy
should	shy'ly
shoul'der	sick
shout	sick'en
shout'ed	sick'le
shout'ing	side
shove	side'board
shov'el	side'-car
shov'el(l)ed	side'-effect
show	side'light
show'down	si'ding
showed	si'dle
show'er	siege
show'ered	sieve
show'ering	sift
show'ing	sift'ed
show'manship	sigh
shown	sighed
show'room	sigh'ing
show'y	sight
shrank	sight'seeing
shrap'nel	sight'seer
shred	sign
shrewd	sig'nal
shriek	sig'natory
shrill	sig'nature

sign'board		sin'ewy	
signed		sin'ful	
sign'er		sin'fully	
signif'icance		sing	
signif'icant		singe	
signif'icantly		singed	
significa'tion		singe'ing	
sig'nified		sing'er	
sig'nify		sing'ing	
sig'nifying		sin'gle	
sign'ing		sin'gle-handed	
sign'post		sin'gular	
sign'writer		singular'ity	
si'lence		sin'ister	
si'lencer		sink	
si'lent		sin'ner	
si'lently		sip	
silhouette'		si'phon	
silicos'is		sip'ping	
silk		sir	
sil'ly		sire	
sil'ver		si'ren	
sil'verware		sir'loin	
sim'ilar		sis'al	
similar'ity		sis'ter	
sim'ilarly		sis'ter-*in*-law	
sim'ile		sit	
simil'itude		site	
sim'mer		sit'ter	
sim'mered		sit'ting	
sim'mering		sit'uate	
sim'per		sit'uated	
sim'pered		situa'tion	
sim'ple		six	
sim'pler		six'fold	
simplic'ity		six'pence	
simplifica'tion		sixteen'	
sim'plify		sixteenth'	
sim'ulate		sixth	
sim'ulated		six'ty	
simulta'neous		size	
sin		size'able	
since		skate	
sincere'		ska'ted	
sincere'ly		ska'ter	
sincer'ity		ska'ting	
si'necure		skel'eton	
sin'ew		sketch	

sketched	
sketch'ily	
sketch'ing	
sketch'y	
skew	
skew'er	
ski	
skid	
skid'ding	
skiff	
skil'ful	
skill	
skilled	
skim	
skimmed	
skimp	
skin	
skinned	
skin'ning	
skip	
skipped	
skip'per	
skir'mish	
skir'mished	
skirt	
skull	
sky	
sky'lark	
sky'light	
sky'scraper	
sky'way	
slab	
slack	
slack'en	
slack'ened	
slag	
slain	
sla'lom	
slam	
slan'der	
slan'dered	
slan'dering	
slan'derous	
slang	
slant	
slant'ed	
slant'ing	
slap	

slapped	
slap'ping	
slash	
slashed	
slash'ing	
slate	
slaugh'ter	
slaugh'tered	
slaugh'ter-	
house	
slave	
sla'very	
sla'vish	
sla'vishly	
slay	
slay'er	
sledge	
sleek	
sleep	
sleep'er	
sleep'ily	
sleep'ing	
sleep'less	
sleep'lessness	
sleep'y	
sleet	
sleeve	
sleigh	
sleight	
slen'der	
slept	
sleuth	
slew	
slice	
sliced	
slick	
slid	
slide	
slide'-rule	
sli'ding	
slight	
slight'est	
slight'ly	
slim	
slime	
sling	
slink	
slip	

slip'per	smat'tering
slip'pery	smear
slip'ping	smeared
slip'road	smear'ing
slip'shod	smell
slit	smelled
slo'gan	smelt
slope	smelt'ed
slot	smelt'er
sloth	smile
sloth'ful	smiled
slot'ted	smi'lingly
slouch	smith
slough (a bog)	smog
slough (a cast skin)	smoke
slov'enly	smo'ker
slow	smooth
slow'ly	smooth'er
slow'ness	smote
slug	smoth'er
slug'gard	smoth'ered
slug'gish	smoul'der
slug'gishly	smoul'dered
sluice	smudge
slum	smug'gle
slum'ber	smug'gled
slum'bered	smug'gler
slum'bering	snack'-bar
slump	snag
slung	snail
slur	snake
slurred	snap
slur'ring	snapped
slush	snap'shot
sly	snare
smack	snared
small	sna'ring
small'er	snarl
small'est	snarled
smart	snatch
smart'en	snatched
smart'er	snatch'ing
smart'est	sneak
smart'ly	sneer
smash	sneered
smashed	sneer'ing
smat'ter	sneeze
	sniff

sniv'el		soiled	
snob		soj'ourn	
snob'bery		sol'ace	
snob'bish		so'lar	
snoop		sold	
snoop'er		sol'der	
snore		sol'dered	
snort		sol'dier	
snow		sole	
snow'drift		sole'ly	
snowed		sol'emn	
snow'fall		solem'nity	
snow'shoes		solemniza'tion	
snow'storm		sol'emnize	
snub		sol'emnly	
snuff		solic'it	
snug		solicita'tion	
so		solic'ited	
soak		solic'itor	
soaked		solic'itous	
soap		solic'itude	
soar		sol'id	
soared		solidar'ity	
sob		solid'ified	
so'ber		solid'ify	
sobri'ety		solid'ity	
so'-called		sol'idly	
socc'er		solil'oquize	
sociabil'ity		solil'oquized	
so'ciable		solil'oquy	
so'cial		sol'itary	
so'cialism		sol'itude	
so'cialist		so'lo	
socialist'ic		so'loist	
soci'ety		solubil'ity	
sociol'ogy		sol'uble	
sociom'etry		solu'tion	
sock		solve	
sock'et		solved	
sod		solv'ency	
so'da		solv'ent	
so'fa		som'bre	
soft		some	
sof'ten		some'body	
sof'tener		some'how	
soft'ly		some'one	
soft'wood		som'ersault	
soil			

some'thing	soured
some'time	south
some'what	south-east'
some'where	south-east'ern
son	south'erly
song	south'ern
song'ster	south'erner
son'ic	south'ward
son'-*in*-law	south-west'
son'net	south-west'ern
sonor'ity	souvenir'
sono'rous	sov'ereign
sono'rously	sov'ereignty
soon	Sov'iet
soon'er	sow (pig)
soot	sow (to scatter)
soothe	sowed
soothed	sow'er
sooth'ing	sow'ing
sop	sown
sophis'ticated	space
sophistica'tion	spaced
soporif'ic	space'-man
sopra'no	space'-ship
sor'did	space'-station
sor'didness	space'-suit
sore	spa'cious
sor'row	spa'ciously
sor'rowful	spade
sor'rowfully	span
sor'rowing	span'gle
sor'ry	Span'iard
sort	span'iel
sort'ed	Span'ish
sort'er	spanned
sort'ing	spar
sought	spare
soul	spared
sound	spar'ing
sound'ed	spar'ingly
sound'er	spark
sound'est	spark'le
sound'ing	spark'led
sound'proof	spark'ling
sound'track	spar'row
soup	sparse
sour	sparse'ly
source	spar'sity

Spar'tan	spell'bound
spasm	spelled
spasmod'ic	spell'ing
spasmod'ically	spelt
spat	spend
spate	spend'ing
spat'ter	spend'thrift
speak	spent
speak'er	sphere
speak'ing	spher'ical
spear	sphinx
spec'ial	spice
spec'ialist	spi'der
special'ity	spike
specializa'tion	spill
spec'ialize	spilled
spec'ially	spilt
spec'ialty	spin
spe'cie	spin'ach
spe'cies	spi'nal
specif'ic	spin'dle
specif'ically	spine
specifica'tion	spin'ster
spec'ified	spi'ral
spec'ify	spire
spec'ifying	spir'it
spec'imen	spir'ited
spe'cious	spir'itual
speck	spit
spec'tacle	spite
spectac'ular	spite'ful
specta'tor	spite'fulness
spec'tre	splash
spectrom'eter	splashed
spec'ulate	splash'ing
spec'ulated	spleen
spec'ulating	splen'did
specula'tion	splen'didly
spec'ulative	splen'dour
spec'ulator	splice
sped	splint
speech	splin'ter
speed	splin'tered
speed'ily	splin'tering
speedom'eter	split
speed'way	splutter'
speed'y	splut'tered
spell	splut'tering

spoil		spur	
spoiled		spu'rious	
spoilt		spurn	
spoke		spurned	
spo'ken		spurn'ing	
spokes'man		spurred	
sponge		spurt	
spon'sor		spy	
spon'sored		spy'ing	
spontane'ity		squab'ble	
sponta'neous		squad	
spool		squad'ron	
spoon		squal'id	
sporad'ic		squall	
sport		squall'y	
sport'ing		squal'or	
sports'man		squan'der	
sports'manship		squan'dered	
sports'wear		squan'dering	
spot		square	
spot'-check		squash	
spot'less		squaw	
spouse		squeak	
spout		squeal	
sprain		squeam'ish	
sprained		squeeze	
sprain'ing		squint	
sprang		squire	
sprawl		squirm	
sprawled		squir'rel	
sprawl'ing		squirt	
spray		stab	
spread		stabbed	
spread'ing		stabil'ity	
sprig		sta'bilize	
spright'ly		sta'bilizer	
spring		sta'ble	
spring'ing		stack	
spring'time		sta'dium	
sprin'kle		staff	
sprin'kled		stag	
sprint		stage	
sprout		stage'craft	
sprout'ed		stag'ger	
spruce		stag'gered	
sprung		stag'gering	
spry		stag'nant	
spun		stagna'tion	

staid		start'ling	
stain		starva'tion	
stained		starve	
stain'less		starved	
stair		starv'ing	
stair'case		state	
stair'way		sta'ted	
stake		state'less	
staked		state'ly	
stale		state'ment	
stalk		state'room	
stalked		states'man	
stalk'er		states'manlike	
stall		states'manship	
stal'wart		stat'ic	
stam'ina		stat'ically	
stam'mer		sta'ting	
stam'mered		sta'tion	
stam'mering		sta'tionary	
stamp		sta'tioned	
stamped		sta'tioner	
stampede'		sta'tionery	
stanch		statis'tical	
stand		statis'tically	
stand'ard		statisti'cian	
standardiza'-		statis'tics	
tion		stat'ue	
stand'ardize		stat'ure	
stand'-by'		sta'tus	
stand'-in		stat'ute	
stand'ing		stat'utory	
stand'point		staunch	
stand'still		stave	
sta'ple		stay	
star		stayed	
starch		stay'ing	
starch'iness		stead	
stare		stead'fast,	
stared		sted'fast	
sta'ring		stead'fastly	
stark		stead'ied	
star'ring		stead'ier	
star'ry		stead'iest	
start		stead'ily	
start'ed		stead'y	
start'er		steak	
start'le		steal	
start'led		stealth	

stealth'y	
steam	
steam'boat	
steamed	
steam'er	
steam'roller	
steam'ship	
steed	
steel	
steel'yard	
steep	
stee'ple	
steer	
steer'age	
steered	
steer'ing	
stem	
stench	
sten'cil	
sten'cilled	
sten'cilling	
stenog'rapher	
stenograph'ic	
stenog'raphy	
sten'tor	
stento'rian	
step	
step'-ladder	
stepped	
step'ping	
step'ping-stone	
ster'eotyped	
ster'ile	
steril'ity	
steriliza'tion	
ster'ilize	
ste'rilizer	
ster'ling	
stern	
stern'er	
stern'est	
stern'ly	
stet	
steth'oscope	
ste'vedore	
stew	
stew'ard	

stew'ardess	
stew'ardship	
stich, stick	
stiff	
stiff'en	
stiff'ened	
sti'fle	
sti'fled	
sti'fling	
stig'ma	
stig'matize	
still	
stim'ulant	
stim'ulate	
stim'ulated	
stim'ulating	
stimula'tion	
stim'ulus	
sting	
stint	
stint'ed	
stint'ing	
sti'pend	
stip'ulate	
stip'ulated	
stip'ulating	
stip'ulation	
stir	
stirred	
stir'ring	
stir'rup	
stitch	
stitched	
stitch'ing	
stock	
stock'broker	
stock'holder	
stock'ing	
stock'ist	
stock'list	
stock'pile	
stock'piling	
stock'taking	
stodg'y	
Stoic	
sto'ical	
sto'icism	
stoke	

stok'er	
stok'ing	
stole	
sto'len	
stol'id	
stom'ach	
stone	
stood	
stooge	
stool	
stoop	
stop	
stop'page	
stop'ping	
stor'age	
store	
stored	
store'keeper	
stor'ing	
storm	
stor'y	
stout	
stout'er	
stout'est	
stout'heart'ed	
stout'ly	
stove	
stow	
stow'age	
stow'away	
stowed	
stow'ing	
strad'dle	
strag'gler	
straight	
straight'away	
straight'en	
straight'ened	
straight'ening	
straight'er	
straight'est	
straightfor'- ward	
strain	
strained	
strain'er	
strain'ing	
strait	

strait'en	
strait'ened	
strand	
strand'ed	
strange	
strange'ly	
stran'ger	
stran'gle	
stran'glehold	
strap	
straphang'er	
stra'ta	
strat'agem	
strateg'ic	
strat'egy	
strat'osphere	
stra'tum	
straw	
straw'berry	
straw'board	
stray	
strayed	
streak	
stream	
streamed	
stream'ing	
stream'line	
street	
strength	
strength'en	
strength'ened	
strength'ening	
stren'uous	
stren'uously	
Streptococ'cus	
streptomy'cin	
stress	
stretch	
stretch'er	
stretch'ing	
strew	
strewed	
strick'en	
strict	
strict'er	
strict'est	
strict'ly	
stric'ture	

stride		
stri'dent		
strife		
strike		
stri'ker		
stri'king		
string		
strin'gency		
strin'gent		
strip		
stripe		
strip'tease		
strive		
strode		
stroke		
stroll		
strolled		
strong		
stron'ger		
stron'gest		
strong'hold		
strong'ly		
strong'minded		
strong'room		
strop		
strove		
struck		
struc'tural		
struc'ture		
strug'gle		
strug'gled		
strug'gling		
strung		
strut		
strut'ted		
strych'nia		
strych'nine		
stub'born		
stub'bornness		
stuc'co		
stuck		
stud		
stud'ded		
stu'dent		
stud'ied		
stu'dio		
stu'dious		
stud'y		

stud'ying		
stuff		
stum'ble		
stum'bled		
stum'bling		
stum'bling-block		
stump		
stumped		
stun		
stunned		
stung		
stunt		
stunt'ed		
stupefac'tion		
stu'pefy		
stupen'dous		
stu'pid		
stupid'ity		
stu'pidly		
stu'por		
stur'dy		
stut'ter		
stut'tered		
stut'tering		
style		
styled		
styl'i		
sty'lish		
sty'lishly		
sty'lo		
suave		
subal'tern		
subaquat'ic		
subcommit'tee		
subdivide'		
subdivi'sion		
subdue'		
subdued'		
subed'it		
sub'hu'man		
{sub'ject, a.		
{subject', v.		
subject'ed, p.p.		
subject'ing		
subjec'tion		
subjec'tive		

subjec'tively
subjoin'
subjoined'
sublet'
sublime'
sublim'ity
sub'marine
submerge'
submers'ible
submis'sion
submiss'ive
submit'
submit'ted
submit'ting
subnor'mal
subor'dinate,
  n., *a.*
subor'dinate, *v.*
subordina'tion
suborn'
subpoe'na
subscribe'
subscribed'
subscri'ber
subscri'bing
subscrip'tion
sub'sequent
sub'sequently
subserv'ient
subside'
subsi'ded
subsi'dence
subsid'iary
sub'sidize
sub'sidized
sub'sidizing
sub'sidy
subsist'
subsist'ed
subsist'ence
subson'ic
sub'stance
substan'tial
substan'-
  tially
substan'tiate
substan'tiated

substantia'-
  tion
sub'stitute
sub'stituted
substitu'tion
subsume'
sub'terfuge
subterra'nean
sub'tle
sub'tlety
subtract'
subtract'ed
subtrac'tion
sub'urb
subur'ban
suburb'ia
sub'urbs
sub'way
succeed'
succeed'ed
succeed'ing
success'
success'ful
success'fully
succes'sion
succes'sive
succes'sively
success'or
succinct'
suc'cour,
  suc'cor
succumb'
succumbed'
such
suck
suck'le
suc'tion
sud'den
sud'denly
sud'denness
sue
sued
suède
su'et
suf'fer
suf'ferance
suf'fered
suf'ferer

suffice'		sun	
sufficed'		sun'bathe	
suffi'ciency		sun'beam	
suffi'cient		sun'burn	
suffi'ciently		sun'burnt	
{suf'fix, *n.*		Sun'day	
{suffix', *v.*		sun'der	
suf'focate		sun'dry	
suf'focated		sung	
suf'focating		sunk	
suffoca'tion		sunk'en	
suf'frage		sun'light	
sug'ar		sun'lit	
suggest'		sun'rise	
suggest'ed		sun'set	
suggest'ing		sun'shine	
sugges'tion		sun'spot	
suggest'ive		sup	
suici'dal		su'per	
su'icide		su'perable	
su'ing		superabun'-	
suit		dance	
suitabil'ity		superabun'-	
suit'able		dant	
suite		superan'nuate	
suit'ed		superan'nua-	
suit'ing		ted	
sulk'y		superannua'-	
sul'len		tion	
sul'lenness		superb'	
sul'phate		supercil'ious	
sul'phide		superfi'cial	
sul'phur		su'perfine	
sulphu'ric		superflu'ity	
sul'tan		super'fluous	
sul'try		superhu'man	
sum		superintend'	
sum'marily		superintend'ed	
sum'marize		superintend'-	
sum'mary		ence	
summed		superintend'-	
sum'mer		ent	
sum'mit		supe'rior	
sum'mon		superior'ity	
sum'moned		super'lative	
sum'mons		super'latively	
sump'tuous		su'permarine	
sump'tuously		su'permarket	

supernat'ural	surf
supersede'	sur'face
superse'ded	surf'-board
superse'ding	sur'feit
superson'ic	sur'feited
supersti'tion	surge
supersti'tious	surged
supervise'	sur'geon
supervised'	sur'gery
supervi'sion	sur'gical
supervi'sor	sur'ly
sup'per	surmise'
supplant'	surmised'
supplant'ed	surmount'
supplant'ing	surmount'able
sup'ple	surmount'ed
sup'plement	surmount'ing
supplemen'tal	sur'name
supplemen'-tary	surpass'
sup'pliant	surpassed'
sup'plicant	sur'plus
sup'plicate	surprise'
supplica'tion	surprised'
supplied'	surpri'sing
supply'	surre'alism
support'	surren'der
support'able	surren'dered
support'ed	surrepti'tious
support'er	surround'
support'ing	surround'ed
suppose'	surround'ing
supposed'	{sur'tax, n.
suppo'sing	{surtax', v.
supposi'tion	sur'vey, n.
suppress'	{survey', v.
suppressed'	surveyed'
suppress'ing	survey'ing
suppres'sion	survey'or
suprem'acy	survi'val
supreme'	survive'
supreme'ly	survived'
{sur'charge, n.	survi'ving
{surcharge', v.	survi'vor
sure	susceptibil'ity
sure'ly	suscep'tible
sur'est	
sure'ty	suscep'tibly
	sus'pect, n.

suspect', v.	swelled	
suspect'ed	swell'ing	
suspend'	swel'ter	
suspend'ed	swel'tered	
suspend'ing	swept	
suspense'	swerve	
suspen'sion	swerved	
suspi'cion	swerv'ing	
suspi'cious	swift	
suspi'ciously	swift'er	
sustain'	swift'est	
sustained'	swift'ly	
sustain'ing	swim	
sus'tenance	swim'mer	
su'ture	swim'ming	
su'tured	swim'mingly	
swag'ger	swin'dle	
swal'low	swin'dled	
swal'lowed	swin'dler	
swal'lowing	swin'dling	
swam	swine	
swamp	swing	
swamped	swing'ing	
swamp'y	Swiss	
swan	switch	
swap	switch'board	
swarm	switched	
swarmed	switch'ing	
swarm'ing	swiv'el	
swarth'y	swoll'en	
swathe	swoon	
sway	swoop	
swayed	sword	
sway'ing	swore	
swear	sworn	
sweat	swung	
sweat'er	syc'amore	
Swede	syllab'ic	
Swe'dish	syl'lable	
sweep	syl'labus	
sweep'er	syl'van	
sweep'ing	sym'bol	
sweet	symbol'ic	
sweet'er	sym'bolize	
sweet'est	symmet'rical	
sweet'ly	symmet'rically	
sweet'ness	sym'metry	
swell	sympathet'ic	

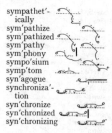

sympathet'-
  ically
sym'pathize
sym'pathized
sym'pathy
sym'phony
sympo'sium
symp'tom
syn'agogue
synchroniza'-
  tion
syn'chronize
syn'chronized
syn'chronizing

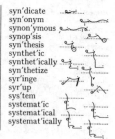

syn'dicate
syn'onym
synon'ymous
synop'sis
syn'thesis
synthet'ic
synthet'ically
syn'thetize
syr'inge
syr'up
sys'tem
systemat'ic
systemat'ical
systemat'ically

T

tab
tab'ernacle
ta'ble
tableau'
ta'ble-cloth
ta'blespoon

ta'blespoon'ful

tab'let
ta'bleware
tab'loid
taboo'
tab'ular
tab'ulate
tab'ulated
tab'ulating
tabula'tion
tab'ulator
tac'it
tac'iturn
tack
tacked
tack'le
tack'led
tact
tact'ful
tact'fully
tac'tical
tactic'ian
tac'tics
tact'less
taff'eta
tag
tail
tail'or
tail'ored
tail'oring
taint
taint'ed
taint'ing

take
ta'ken
take'-over
ta'king
talc
tale
tal'ent
tal'ented
tal'isman
talk
talk'ative
talk'er
talk'ing
tall
tall'er
tallest
tal'lied
tal'low
tal'ly
tame
tamed
ta'mer
tam'per
tam'pered
tam'pering
tan
tan'dem
tan'gent
tan'gible
tan'gle
tan'go
tank
tank'ard
tan'ker
tan'ner
tan'nery
tan'nic
tan'nin
tan'talize
tan'talizing

tan'tamount	taunt'ing
tan'trum	taut
tap	tav'ern
tape	taw'dry
ta'per	taw'ny
tape'-record'er	tax
ta'pering	tax'able
tap'estry	taxa'tion
tapio'ca	taxed
tapped	tax'i
tap'ping	tax'icab
tar	tax'payer
tar'dily	tea
tar'diness	teach
tar'dy	teach'er
tare	teach'ing
tar'get	tea'cup
tar'iff	teak
tar'mac	team
tar'nish	tea'pot
tar'nished	tear, *n.*
tarpau'lin	tear, *v.*
tar'ried	tear'ful
tar'ring	tear'ing
tar'ry, *adj.*	tease
tar'ry, *v.*	tea'spoon
tart	tea'spoonful
tar'tan	tech'nical
tar'tar	technical'ity
tartar'ic	tech'nically
task	technique'
tas'sel	technol'ogist
taste	technol'ogy
ta'sted	te'dious
taste'ful	te'diously
taste'fully	te'dium
taste'less	tee
taste'lessness	teem
ta'sting	teemed
ta'sty	teem'ing
tat'ter	teen'age
tat'tered	teen'ager
tat'tle	teeth
tattoo'	teethe
tattooed'	teeto'tal
taught	teeto'taler,
taunt	teeto'taller
taunt'ed	

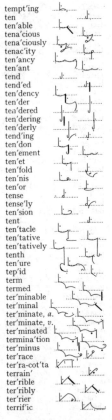

tel'ecast	tempt'ing
telegen'ic	ten
tel'egram	ten'able
tel'egraph	tena'cious
telegraph'ic	tena'ciously
teleg'raphist	tenac'ity
teleg'raphy	ten'ancy
telep'athy	ten'ant
tel'ephone	tend
telephon'ic	tend'ed
teleph'onist	ten'dency
teleph'ony	ten'der
tele'photo	ten'dered
tel'eprinter	ten'dering
teleprompt'er	ten'derly
tel'escope	tend'ing
telescop'ic	ten'don
tele'type	ten'ement
tel'eview	ten'et
tele'vise	ten'fold
tel'evision	ten'nis
tell	ten'or
tell'er	tense
telling	tense'ly
tell'-tale	ten'sion
temer'ity	tent
tem'per	ten'tacle
tem'perament	ten'tative
tempera-men'tal	ten'tatively
tempera-men'tally	tenth
tem'perance	ten'ure
tem'perate	tep'id
tem'perately	term
tem'perature	termed
tem'pered	ter'minable
tem'pering	ter'minal
tem'pest	ter'minate, a.
tempes'tuous	ter'minate, v.
tem'ple	ter'minated
tem'poral	termina'tion
tem'porarily	ter'minus
tem'porary	ter'race
tempt	ter'ra-cot'ta
tempta'tion	terrain'
tempt'ed	ter'rible
	ter'ribly
	ter'rier
	terrif'ic

ter'rified
ter'rify
territo'rial
ter'ritory
ter'ror
ter'rorism
ter'rorize
terse
terse'ly
terylene'
test
tes'tament
testamen'tary
testa'tor
testa'trix
test'ed
test'er
tes'tified
tes'tify
testimo'nial
tes'timony
test'ing
tes'ty
teth'er
teth'ered
text
text'book
tex'tile
tex'ture
than
thank
thanked
thank'ful
thank'fully
thank'fulness
thank'ing
thank'less
thanks
thanks'giving
that
thatch
thatched
thaw
thawed
the
the'atre,
   the'ater
theat'rical

theft
their
theirs
them
theme
themselves'
then
thence
thenceforth'
thencefor'ward
theolog'ical
theolog'-
   ically
theol'ogist
theol'ogy
the'orem
theoret'ical
theoret'ically
the'orist
the'orize
the'ory
there
there'about
thereaf'ter
thereat'
thereby'
there'for
there'fore
therefrom'
therein'
thereof'
thereon'
thereout'
thereto'
thereupon'
therewith'
therm
thermion'ic
thermom'eter
ther'mos
ther'mostat
these
the'sis
they
thick
thick'en
thick'ened
thick'ening

thick'er	
thick'et	
thick'ly	
thick'ness	
thief	
thieves	
thigh	
thim'ble	
thin	
thine	
thing	
think	
think'er	
think'ing	
thin'ly	
thinned	
thin'ner	
third	
third'ly	
third'-rate'	
thirds	
thirst	
thirst'ed	
thirst'ing	
thirst'y	
thirteen'	
thirteenth'	
thir'tieth	
thir'ty	
this	
this'tle	
thorn	
thorn'y	
thor'ough	
thor'oughbred	
thor'oughfare	
thor'oughly	
thor'oughness	
those	
thou	
though	
thought	
thought'ful	
thought'fully	
thought'ful- ness	
thought'less	
thought'lessly	

thought'less- ness	
thou'sand	
thou'sandfold	
thrash	
thrashed	
thrash'ing	
thread	
thread'bare	
thread'ed	
thread'ing	
threat	
threat'en	
threat'ened	
three	
three- quarters	
thresh	
thresh'old	
threw	
thrice	
thrift	
thrift'y	
thrill	
thrilled	
thrill'er	
thrill'ing	
thrive	
thri'ving	
throat	
throb	
throbbed	
throb'bing	
throne	
throng	
thronged	
throng'ing	
throt'tle	
through	
throughout'	
throw	
throw'back	
throw'ing	
thrown	
thrust	
thrust'ing	
thud	
thumb	

thump	
thumped	
thun'der	
thun'dered	
Thurs'day	
thus	
thwart	
thwart'ed	
tick'et	
tick'le	
ti'dal	
tide	
ti'ded	
ti'dings	
ti'dy	
tie	
tied	
tier	
ti'ger	
tight	
tight'en	
tight'ened	
tight'ening	
tight'ly	
tight'ness	
tile	
tiled	
till, *n.* and *v.*	
till, *prep.*	
tilt	
tilt'ed	
tilt'ing	
tim'ber	
time	
time'keeper	
time'table	
tim'id	
timid'ity	
tim'idly	
tim'orous	
tin	
tinc'ture	
tinge	
tin'gle	
tin'kle	
tinned	
tin'plate	
tin'sel	

tint	
tint'ed	
tint'ing	
ti'ny	
tip	
tip'off	
tipped	
tip'ping	
tirade'	
tire	
tired	
tire'less	
tire'some	
tir'o	
tis'sue	
Titan'ic	
tit'-bit	
tithe	
ti'tle	
tit'ter	
tit'ular	
to	
toast	
toast'ed	
toast'ing	
tobac'co	
tobac'conist	
tobog'gan	
today'	
toe	
tof'fee, tof'fy	
togeth'er	
toil	
toiled	
toi'let	
tok'en	
told	
tol'erable	
tol'erably	
tol'erance	
tol'erant	
tol'erate	
tol'erated	
tol'erating	
tolera'tion	
toll	
tolled	

toma'to	tot'ter
tomb	touch
tomb'stone	touched
tomor'row	touch'ing
ton	tough
tone	tough'en
tongs	tough'er
tongue	tough'est
ton'ic	tough'ness
tonight'	tour
ton'nage	tour'ing
too	tour'ism
took	tour'ist
tool	tour'nament
tooth	tour'ney
tooth'ache	tout
top	tout'ed
to'paz	tout'ing
top'-heavy	tow
top'ic	*to'ward*
top'ical	*to'wards*
top'ple	towed
top'pled	tow'el
top'pling	tow'er
torch	tow'ered
tore	tow'ering
{tor'ment, *n.*	tow'ing
{torment', *v.*	town
torment'ed	town'-clerk'
torment'ing	town'ship
torn	towns'man
torna'do	tox'ic
torpe'do	toy
tor'pid	toyed
tor'rent	trace
torren'tial	trace'able
tor'rid	traced
tor'toise	tra'cer
tor'tuous	tra'cing
tor'ture	track
tor'tured	tracked
tor'turing	track'less
toss	tract
tossed	tract'able
toss'ing	trac'tion
to'tal	trac'tor
to'tally	*trade*
tote	*tra'ded*

trade'-mark
tra'der
trades'man
trades-u'nion

trades-u'nion-
ism
trade-u'nion
tra'ding
tradi'tion
tradi'tional
tradi'tionally
traf'fic
trag'edy
trag'ic
trag'ically
trail
trail'er
trail'ing
train
trainee'
train'er
train'ing
trait
trai'tor
tram
tramp
tramped
tramp'ing
tram'ple
tram'pled
tram'pling
trance
tran'quil
tranquil'lity
transact'
transact'ed
transact'ing
transac'tion
transatlan'tic
transcend
transcend'ed
transcend'ence
transcend'ent
transcribe'
transcribed'
tran'script
transcrip'tion

(trans'fer, *n.*
(transfer', *v.*
trans'ferable
trans'ference
transferred'

transfix'
transform'

transforma'-
tion
transform'er

transgress'
transgressed'
transgress'ing
transgres'sion
tranship'
tranship'ment
tran'sient
transist'or
trans'it
transi'tion
transi'tional
trans'itory
translate'
transla'ted
transla'ting
transla'tion
transla'tor
transmis'sion
transmit'
transmit'ted
transmit'ter
transmit'ting
transpa'rent
transpire'
transpired'
transpi'ring
transplant'
(trans'port, *n.*
(transport', *v.*
transporta'-
tion
transport'ed
transpose'
transship'
transship'ment
trap

trap'-door'	tri'bal
trapeze'	tribe
trapped	tribula'tion
trap'ping	tribu'nal
trash	trib'une
trav'el	trib'utary
trav'elled,	trib'ute
trav'eled	tri'ceps
trav'eller,	trick
trav'eler	tricked
trav'elogue	trick'ery
trav'erse	trick'le
trav'ersed	trick'led
treach'erous	trick'y
treach'ery	tried
treac'le	trien'nial
tread	tri'fle
tread'ing	tri'fled
trea'son	tri'fling
treas'ure	trig'ger
treas'urer	trim
treas'ury	trim'ly
treat	trimmed
treat'ed	trin'ity
treat'ing	trin'ket
trea'tise	tri'o
treat'ment	trip
trea'ty	tripe
treb'le	trip'le
tree	trip'lex
trel'lis	trip'licate, *n.*
trem'ble	*a.*
trem'bled	trip'licate, *v.*
trem'bling	trite
tremen'dous	trite'ly
trem'or	trite'ness
trem'ulous	tri'umph
trench	trium'phal
trench'ant	trium'phant
trend	trium'phantly
tres'pass	tri'umphed
tres'passed	triv'ial
tres'passer	trivial'ity
tres'passing	trod
tress	trodd'en
tri'al	trol'ley
tri'angle	troop
trian'gular	troop'er

tro′phy		try	
trop′ical		try′ing	
trot		try′-*on*	
trot′ted		tryst	
trot′ting		tub	
troub′le		tube	
troub′led		tuber′cular	
troub′lesome		tuberculo′sis	
troub′ling		tuber′culous	
troub′lous		tu′bing	
trough		tu′bular	
trou′sers		tuck	
trousseau′		Tu′dor	
trout		Tues′day	
trow′el		tuft	
tru′ant		tug	
truce		tui′tion	
truck		tu′lip	
tru′culence		tum′ble	
tru′culent		tum′bled	
trudge		tum′bler	
trudged		tu′mult	
trudg′ing		tumul′tuous	
true		tune	
tru′est		tuned	
tru′ism		tune′ful	
trump		tune′fully	
trump′et		tu′ner	
trump′eter		tu′nic	
trun′dle		tu′ning	
trunk		tun′nel	
trunk′-call		tur′bine	
truss		tur′bulent	
trust		turf	
trust′ed		Turk	
trustee′		tur′key	
trust′ful		tur′moil	
trust′fully		turn	
trust′ing		turned	
trust′ingly		turn′er	
trust′worthi-		turn′ing	
ness		turn′ing-point	
trust′worthy		tur′nip	
trust′y		turn′over	
truth		turn′stile	
truth′ful		turn′table	
truth′fulness		tur′pentine	
truths		tur′ret	

tur'tle		*two*-seater	
tusk		*two*-some	
tus'sle		ty'ing	
tu'tor		type	
tuto'rial		type'script	
tu'tors		type'writer	
tweed		type'writing	
twee'zers		type'written	
twelfth		ty'phoid	
twelve		typhoon'	
twen'tieth		typ'ical	
twen'ty		typ'ified	
twice		typ'ify	
twig		ty'pist	
twi'light			
twill		typograph'ic	
twin		typograph'ical	
twine		typog'raphy	
twinge		typol'ogy	
twi'ning		tyran'nic	
twin'kle		tyran'nical	
twin'kled		tyran'nically	
twin'kling		tyr'annize	
twist		tyr'annized	
twist'ed		tyr'annous	
twist'ing		tyr'anny	
twitch		ty'rant	
two		tyre	
two'fold		ty'ro	
		ty'rotox'icon	

U

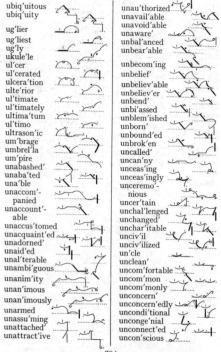

ubiq'uitous
ubiq'uity

ug'lier
ug'liest
ug'ly
ukule'le
ul'cer
ul'cerated
ulcera'tion
ulte'rior
ul'timate
ul'timately
ultima'tum
ul'timo
ultrason'ic
um'brage
umbrel'la
um'pire
unabashed'
unaba'ted
una'ble
unaccom'-
  panied
unaccount'-
  able
unaccus'tomed
unacquaint'ed
unadorned'
unaid'ed
unal'terable
unambi'guous
unanim'ity
unan'imous
unan'imously
unarmed'
unassu'ming
unattached'
unattract'ive

unau'thorized
unavail'able
unavoid'able
unaware'
unbal'anced
unbear'able
unbecom'ing
unbelief'
unbeliev'able
unbeliev'er
unbend'
unbi'assed
unblem'ished
unborn'
unbound'ed
unbrok'en
uncalled'
uncan'ny
unceas'ing
unceas'ingly
unceremo'-
  nious
uncer'tain
unchal'lenged
unchanged'
unchar'itable
unciv'il
unciv'ilized
un'cle
unclean'
uncom'fortable
uncom'mon
uncom'monly
unconcern'
unconcern'edly
uncondi'tional
unconge'nial
unconnect'ed
uncon'scious

204

unconstitu'-tional	understate'ment
unconstitu'-tionally	understood'
uncontrol'lable	un'derstudy
uncontrolled'	undertake'
unconven'tional	un'dertone
uncouth'	un'derwear
uncov'er	un'derworld
uncul'tivated	un'derwriter
uncut'	undeserved'
unda'ted	undesir'able
undaunt'ed	undeterred'
undeci'ded	undisclosed'
undefend'ed	undisturbed'
undefiled'	undivi'ded
undefined'	undo'
undeliv'ered	undoubt'ed
undeni'able	undoubt'edly
un'der	undress'
un'dercarriage	undue'
un'dercoat	un'dulating
un'dercurrent	undu'ly
un'derdog	unearned'
under-es'timate, n.	uneas'ily
under-es'timate, v.	uneas'y
	uneconom'ic
under-es'timated	unemploy'able
undergo'	unemployed'
undergrad'uate	unemploy'-ment
un'derground	une'qual
un'dergrowth	une'qualled
un'derhand	uner'ring
underline'	uner'ringly
underly'ing	une'ven
underneath'	une'venly
un'der-nourished	unevent'ful
un'derpass	unexam'pled
un'der-pri'vileged	unexpect'ed
underrate'	unexpect'edly
under-sec'retary	unfail'ing
un'derstaffed	unfair'
understand'	unfaith'ful
	unfamil'iar
	unfash'ionable
	unfa'vourable
	unfeel'ing

unfeigned'	u'nison
unfert'ilized	u'nit
unfin'ished	unite'
unfit'	uni'ted
unflag'ging	u'nity
unflat'tering	univer'sal
unfold'	universal'ity
unforeseen'	univer'sally
unforgett'able	u'niverse
unfor'tunate	univer'sity
unfor'tunately	unjust'
unfound'ed	unjus'tifiable
unfriend'ly	unjus'tified
unfulfilled'	unkind'
unfurl'	unknown'
unfurled'	unlaw'ful
unfur'nished	unless'
ungen'tlemanly	unlike'
ungov'ernable	unlike'ly
ungra'cious	unlim'ited
ungrate'ful	unload'
unguard'ed	unlock'
unhap'pily	unluck'ily
unhap'py	unluck'y
unharmed'	unman'nerly
unhealth'y	unmind'ful
unhes'itatingly	unmista'kable
unhook'	unmit'igated
unhurt'	unmoved'
unhygien'ic	unnat'ural
uni'fied	unnec'essarily
u'niform	unnec'essary
uniform'ity	unno'ticed
u'niformly	unobtain'able
u'nify	unoffi'cial
unilat'eral	unor'ganized
unimpaired'	
unimpor'tant	unorth'odox
unin'fluenced	unpaid'
uninformed'	unpal'atable
unintel'ligible	unpar'alleled
uninten'tional	unpleas'ant
uninterrupt'ed	unpleas'antly
u'nion	unpop'ular
U'nionist	unprec'edented
unique'	unprej'udiced

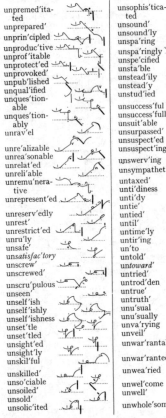
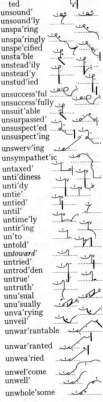

unpremed'ita-
  ted
unprepared'
unprin'cipled
unproduc'tive
unprof'itable
unprotect'ed
unprovoked'
unpub'lished
unqual'ified
unques'tion-
  able
unques'tion-
  ably
unrav'el

unre'alizable
unrea'sonable
unrelat'ed
unreli'able
unremu'nera-
  tive
unrepresent'ed

unreserv'edly
unrest'
unrestrict'ed
unru'ly
unsafe'
un*satisfac'tory*
unscrew'
unscrewed'

unscru'pulous
unseen'
unself'ish
unself'ishly
unself'ishness
unset'tle
unset'tled
unsight'ed
unsight'ly
unskil'ful

unskilled'
unso'ciable
unsoiled'
unsold'
unsolic'ited

unsophis'tica-
  ted
unsound'
unsound'ly
unspa'ring
unspa'ringly
unspe'cified
unsta'ble
unstead'ily
unstead'y
unstud'ied

unsuccess'ful
unsuccess'fully
unsuit'able
unsurpassed'
unsuspect'ed
unsuspect'ing

unswerv'ing
unsympathet'ic

untaxed'
unti'diness
unti'dy
untie'
untied'
until'
untime'ly
untir'ing
un'to
untold'
un*toward'*
untried'
untrod'den
untrue'
untruth'
unu'sual
unu'sually
unva'rying
unveil'
unwar'rantable

unwar'ranted

unwea'ried

unwel'come
unwell'
unwhole'some

unwield'y	ur'gent
unwil'ling	ur'gently
unwil'lingly	urn
unwise'	us
unwise'ly	u'sable
unwit'tingly	u'sage
unwork'able	use
unwor'thy	used
unwrit'ten	use'ful
unyield'ing	use'fully
up	use'fulness
up'bringing	use'less
upheav'al	use'lessly
upheave'	use'lessness
upheld'	u'ser
uphill'	ush'er
uphold'	ush'ered
uphold'ing	usherette'
uphol'ster	u'sing
uphol'sterer	u'sual
uphol'stery	u'sually
uplift'	u'surer
upon'	usurp'
up'per	u'sury
up'permost	uten'sil
up'right'	util'ity
up'roar	utiliza'tion
uproar'ious	u'tilize
uproot'	u'tilized
upset'	u'tilizing
up'surge	ut'most
up'swing	Uto'pia
up'wards	ut'ter
ur'ban	ut'terance
urbane'	ut'tered
urban'ity	ut'tering
ur'chin	ut'terly
urge	ut'termost
ur'gency	u'vula

V

va'cancy
va'cant
vacate'
vaca'ted
vaca'ting
vaca'tion
vac'cinate
vac'cinated
vaccina'tion
vac'cine
vac'illate
vac'illated
vac'illating
vacilla'tion
vac'uous
vac'uum
vag'abond
vaga'ry
va'grancy
va'grant
vague
vague'ly
vain
vain'ly
vale
valedic'tory
val'ency
val'et
val'iant
val'iantly
val'id
val'idate
valid'ity
valise'
val'ley
val'orous
val'our
val'uable
valua'tion
val'ue

val'ued
valve
valv'ular
vamp
vam'pire
van
vanil'la
van'ish
van'ished
van'ishing
van'ity
van'quish
van'tage
vap'id
vap'orizer
va'pour,
   va'por
va'riable
va'riance
va'riant
varia'tion
va'ried
vari'ety
va'rious
var'nish
var'nishing
va'ry
va'rying
vase
Vas'eline
vas'sal
vast
vast'ly
vat
Vat'ican
vaude'ville
vault
vault'ed
vault'ing
vaunt

vaunt'ed		ven'ue	
veal		vera'cious	
veer		verac'ity	
veered		veran'dah	
veer'ing		verb	
veg'etable		ver'bal	
vegeta'rian		verba'tim	
		ver'biage	
vegeta'rianism		verbose'	
veg'etate		verbos'ity	
vegeta'tion		ver'dant	
ve'hemence		ver'dict	
ve'hement		ver'dure	
ve'hemently		verge	
ve'hicle		verifica'tion	
vehic'ular		ver'ified	
veil		ver'ify	
veiled		ver'ily	
vein		ver'itable	
vel'lum		vermil'ion	
veloc'ity		ver'min	
velour'		ver'satile	
vel'vet		versatil'ity	
velveteen'		verse	
vend'er,		ver'sion	
vend'or		ver'sus	
vendet'ta		ver'tebrae	
vend'or		ver'tical	
(*legal term*)		*ver'y*	
veneer'		ves'sel	
ven'erable		vest	
ven'erate		vest'ed	
venera'tion		ves'tibule	
Vene'tian		ves'tige	
ven'geance		vest'ment	
ve'nial		ves'try	
ven'ison		ves'ture	
ven'om		vet'eran	
ven'omous		vet'erinary	
vent		ve'to	
ven'tilate		vex	
ven'tilated		vexa'tion	
ventila'tion		vexa'tious	
ven'tilator		vexed	
ven'ture		vi'a	
ven'tured		vi'aduct	
ven'turesome		vi'al	
ven'turing		vi'brant	

vi′brate	viola′tion	
vi′brated	vi′olence	
vibra′tion	vi′olent	
vic′ar	vi′olently	
vica′rious	vi′olet	
vice	violin′	
vice-chair′man	violin′ist	
vice-pres′ident	vi′per	
vice-prin′cipal	vir′gin	
	vir′ile	
vic′e ver′sa	viril′ity	
vicin′ity	vir′tual	
vic′ious	vir′tue	
vic′iously	virtuos′ity	
vicis′situde	vir′tuous	
vic′tim	vir′ulence	
victimiza′tion	vir′ulent	
vic′tor	vi′sa	
victo′rious	vis′age	
vic′tory	vis′cous	
vict′uals	vi′sé	
vid′eo	visibil′ity	
vie	vis′ible	
view	vi′sion	
viewed	vi′sionary	
vig′il	vis′it	
vig′ilance	visita′tion	
vig′ilant	vis′ited	
vig′orous	vis′iting	
vig′our	vis′itor	
vile	vis′ta	
vil′la	vis′ual	
vil′lage	visualiza′tion	
vil′lain	vis′ualize	
vil′lainous	vi′tal	
vil′lainy	vital′ity	
vim	vi′tally	
vin′dicate	vi′tamin	
vin′dicated	vi′tiate	
vindica′tion	vi′tiated	
vindic′tive	vitriol′ic	
vindic′tively	vitu′perate	
vine	vitupera′tion	
vin′egar	viva′cious	
vine′yard	vivac′ity	
vin′tage	viv′id	
vi′olate	viv′idly	
vi′olated	vivisec′tion	

vocab'ulary	volunteer'
vo'cal	volunteered'
vo'calist	volunteer'ing
vocaliza'tion	vora'cious
vcca'tion	vo'tary
voca'tional	vote
vocif'erous	vo'ted
vod'ka	vo'ter
vogue	vouch
voice	vouch'er
void	vouchsafe
vol'atile	vow
vol'-au-vent'	vowed
	vow'el
volcan'ic	voy'age
	vul'canite
volca'no	
vol'ley	vul'canize
volt	vul'gar
volt'age	vulgar'ity
volubil'ity	vul'garly
vol'uble	
vol'ume	vulnerabil'ity
volu'minous	vul'nerable
vol'untarily	vul'ture
vol'untary	vy'ing

W

wad		
wad'ding		
wade		
wa'ded		
wa'ding		
wa'fer		
waf'fle		
waft		
waft'ed		
wag		
wage		
wage'-freeze		
wa'ger		
wag'on, wag'gon		
waif		
wail		
wailed		
wain'scot		
wain'scotting		
waist		
waist'coat		
wait		
wait'ed		
wait'er		
wait'ing-list		
wait'ing-room		
wait'ress		
waive		
wake		
wake'ful		
wake'fulness		
wa'ken		
wa'kening		
walk		
walked		
walk'er		
walk'ing		
walk'ing-stick		
walk'-out		

walk'-over	
wall	
wal'let	
wal'low	
wall'paper	
wal'nut	
wal'rus	
waltz	
waltzed	
wan	
wand	
wan'der	
wan'dered	
wan'derer	
wan'dering	
wane	
want	
want'ed	
wan'ton	
war	
war'ble	
ward	
ward'en	
ward'er	
ward'robe	
ware'house	
wares	
war'fare	
war'ily	
war'like	
warm	
warmed	
warm'er	
warm'est	
warm'-hearted	
warmth	
warn	
warned	
warn'ing	
warn'ingly	

warp	
war'rant	
war'ranted	
war'ranty	
war'rior	
war'ship	
wa'ry	
was	
wash	
wash'able	
washed	
wash'er	
wash'ing	
wash'out	
wasp	
waste	
wast'ed	
waste'ful	
waste'fully	
wa'sting	
watch	
watched	
watch'er	
watch'ful	
watch'fulness	
watch'ing	
watch'man	
wa'ter	
wa'terfall	
wa'terfront	
wa'termark	
wa'termelon	
wa'terproof	
wa'tershed	
wa'tertight	
watt	
wave	
waved	
wave'length	
wa'ver	
wa'vered	
wa'vering	
wa'ving	
wa'vy	
wax	
way	
way'farer	

way'faring	
way'side	
we	
weak	
weak'en	
weak'er	
weak'ness	
weal	
wealth	
wealth'ier	
wealth'iest	
wealth'y	
weap'on	
wear	
wear'able	
wear'er	
wear'ied	
wear'ing	
wear'isome	
wear'y	
wear'ying	
weath'er	
weath'erproof	
weave	
weav'er	
weav'ing	
web	
wed'ding	
wedge	
wedged	
wedg'ing	
Wednes'day	
weed	
week	
week'day	
week-end'	
week'ly	
weep	
weigh	
weighed	
weigh'ing	
weight	
weight'y	
weir	
weird	
wel'come	
wel'comed	
wel'coming	

weld		which	
weld'ed		whichev'er	
weld'ing		whiff	
wel'fare		while	
well		whiled	
well-known'		whilst	
well-mean'ing		whim	
Welsh		whim'per	
wel'ter		whim'pered	
went		whim'pering	
wept		whim'sical	
were		whine	
west		whined	
west'erly		whi'ning	
west'ern		whip	
west'ward		whirl	
wet		whirled	
whale		whirl'ing	
wharf		whirl'pool	
wharf'age		whirl'wind	
what		whis'key,	
what'ever		whis'ky	
whatsoev'er		whis'per	
wheat		whis'pered	
wheel		whis'pering	
wheel'-base		whist	
wheeled		whis'tle	
when		whis'tled	
whence		whit	
whenev'er		white	
whensoev'er		whith'er	
where		whithersoev'er	
where'abouts		whit'tle	
whereas'		whiz	
whereat'		who	
whereby'		whoev'er	
where'fore		whole	
where*in*		whole'heart'ed	
whereinsoev'er		whole-	
		heart'edly	
where*of*'		whole'sale	
where*on*'		whole'some	
wheresoev'er		whol'ly	
where*to*'		whom	
whereupon'		whoop	
wherev'er		whose	
wherewithal'		whosoev'er	
wheth'er		why	

wick			wine'-glass		
wick'ed			wing		
wick'er			wink		
wick'et			win'ner		
wide			win'ning		
wide'ly			win'some		
wi'den			win'ter		
wi'dened			win'terly		
wi'dening			win'try		
wi'der			wipe		
wide'spread			wiped		
wid'ow			wi'ping		
wid'ower			wire		
width			wired		
wield			wire'less		
wife			wir'y		
wig			wis'dom		
wild			wise		
wild'er			wise'ly		
wil'derness			wi'ser		
wild'est			wi'sest		
wild'ly			wish		
wile			wished		
wil'ful			wish'ing		
wil'fully			wist'ful		
wil'fulness			wist'fully		
will			wit		
willed			*with*		
will'ing			withal'		
wil'lingly			withdraw'		
wil'low			withdraw'al		
wilt			withdrawn'		
wi'ly			withdrew'		
win			with'er		
wince			with'ered		
winced			withheld'		
wind, *n.*			withhold'		
wind, *v.*			within'		
wind'fall			*without'*		
wind'ing			withstand'		
win'dow			withstood'		
win'dow-dressing			wit'ness		
wind'screen			wit'ticism		
wind'-tunnel			wit'ty		
wind'ward			wiz'ard		
wine			wob'ble		
wine'-cellar			wob'bled		
			wob'bling		

woke		wor'sen	
wolf		wor'ship	
wom'an		worst	
wom'anhood		wors'ted	
wom'anly		worth	
wom'en		wor'thier	
won		wor'thiest	
won'der		wor'thily	
won'dered		worth'less	
won'derful		worth'lessness	
won'derfully			
won'dering		worthwhile'	
won'deringly		wor'thy	
won'drous		*would*	
won'drously		*would'-be*	
won't		wound, *n., v.*	
wont		wound, *v.*	
wont'ed		wound'ing	
wood		wove	
wood'en		wo'ven	
wood'work		wran'gle	
wool		wrap	
wool'len		wrapped	
wooll'ies		wrap'per	
wool'sack		wrap'ping	
word		wrath	
word'ed		wrath'ful	
word'ing		wreath	
word'y		wreathe	
wore		wreck	
work		wreck'age	
work'able		wrecked	
worked		wreck'ing	
work'er		wrench	
work'less		wrenched	
		wrench'ing	
work'man		wrest	
work'manship		wres'tle	
work'shop		wres'tled	
world		wrest'ling	
world'ly		wretch	
world'wide		wretch'ed	
worm		wretch'edness	
worn		wrig'gle	
wor'ried		wright	
wor'ry		wring	
wor'rying		wring'er	
worse		wrin'kle	

wrist		
wrist'let		
wrist'watch		
writ		
write		
wri'ter		
write'-up		
writhe		
writhed		
wri'ting		
writ'ten		

wrong		
wronged		
wrong'ful		
wrong'fully		
wrong'ly		
wrote		
wroth		
wrought'		
wrought'-iron'		
wrung		
wry		

X

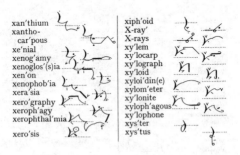

xan'thium
xantho-
  car'pous
xe'nial
xenog'amy
xenoglos'(s)ia
xen'on
xenophob'ia
xera'sia
xero'graphy
xeroph'agy
xerophthal'mia

xero'sis

xiph'oid
X-ray'
X-rays
xy'lem
xy'locarp
xy'lograph
xy'loid
xyloi'din(e)
xylom'eter
xy'lonite
xyloph'agous
xy'lophone
xys'ter
xys'tus

Y

yacht		
yacht'ing		
yank		
yard		
yarn		
yawn		
yawned		
yawn'ing		
ye		
yea		
year		
year'-book		
year'ly		
yearn		
yearned		
yearn'ing		
yeast		
yell		
yel'low		
yelp		
yelped		
yelp'ing		
yes		
yes'terday		

yet		
yew		
Yid'dish		
yield		
yield'ed		
yo'ghourt		
yoke		
yo'kel		
yolk		
yon'der		
you		
young		
young'er		
young'est		
young'ster		
your		
*your*self'		
*your*selves'		
youth		
youth'ful		
youth'-		
fulness		
youths		
Yule		
Yule'tide		

Z

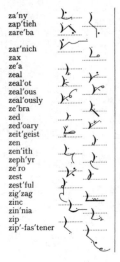
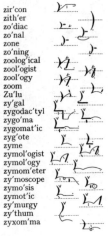

za'ny
zap'tieh
zare'ba

zar'nich
zax
ze'a
zeal
zeal'ot
zeal'ous
zeal'ously
ze'bra
zed
zed'oary
zeit'geist
zen
zen'ith
zeph'yr
ze'ro
zest
zest'ful
zig'zag
zinc
zin'nia
zip
zip'-fas'tener

zir'con
zith'er
zo'diac
zo'nal
zone
zo'ning
zoolog'ical
zool'ogist
zool'ogy
zoom
Zu'lu
zy'gal
zygodac'tyl
zygo'ma
zygomat'ic
zyg'ote
zyme
zymol'ogist
zymol'ogy
zymom'eter
zy'moscope
zymo'sis
zymot'ic
zy'murgy
zy'thum
zyxom'ma